TEACHING TASTE

Karen Wistoft
Lars Qvortrup

TEACHING TASTE

Karen Wistoft
Lars Qvortrup

COMMON
GROUND

First published in 2019
as part of the Food Studies Book Imprint
http://doi.org/10.18848/978-1-86335-164-5/CGP (Full Book)

BISAC Codes: EDU000000, EDU040000, EDU037000

Common Ground Research Networks
2001 South First Street, Suite 202
University of Illinois Research Park
Champaign, IL
61820

Library of Congress Cataloging-in-Publication Data

Names: Wistoft, Karen, author. | Qvortrup, Lars, author.
Title: Teaching taste / Karen Wistoft, Lars Qvortrup.
Other titles: Smagens didaktik. English
Description: Champaign, IL : Common Ground Research Networks, 2019. |
  Includes bibliographical references. | Summary: "How we taste and eat is
  just as central in a civilization perspective as what we know and think.
  Meal communities are important contributors to the creation of a
  community of opinions based on sense, emotion and taste. This is the
  reason for writing Teaching Taste. The historical part analyses Danish
  children's cookbooks. When did the view of taste change from a norm that
  was met to a sense and ability that everyone, including children,
  possesses? The systematic part identifies seven dimensions of taste:
  pleasant taste, healthy taste, sensed taste, moral taste, religious
  taste, loving taste and trendy taste and how to teach them. The didactic
  part answers how can we teach about, through and for taste. The book is
  written for teachers, trainee teachers and students on courses in Home
  Economics, Food Knowledge and Food Education. The book ends with a
  ready-to-use teaching handout"-- Provided by publisher.
Identifiers: LCCN 2019032185 (print) | LCCN 2019032186 (ebook) | ISBN
  9781863351621 (hardback) | ISBN 9781863351638 (paperback) | ISBN
  9781863351645 (pdf)
Subjects: LCSH: Food habits--Denmark--History. | Cooking, Danish--History.
  | Cooking--Denmark--Social aspects. | Taste. | Denmark--Social life and
  customs.
Classification: LCC GT2853.D4 W13 2019 (print) | LCC GT2853.D4 (ebook) |
  DDC 394.1/209489--dc23
LC record available at https://lccn.loc.gov/2019032185
LC ebook record available at https://lccn.loc.gov/2019032186

Table of Contents

Introduction

In Denmark, recent years have seen a 'turn' in food education as well as in Home Economics in primary and lower secondary school. This turn has also included health education, home and consumer studies, education towards sustainable development and other further education courses. Previously, the primary focus was on practical skills, health and nutrition. Today, there is more focus on taste as a quality of food and meals, and on health as more than something bodily or nutritional: health is seen in a broader perspective that includes social thriving, well-being, etc. Food quality is also defined more broadly: previously, it was mainly about nutritional value and labelling; today, food quality chiefly concerns sustainability and taste.

We have not seen this turn so markedly in other countries. There is a strong interest in taste education in North European countries. In other countries, there is still a focus on nutrition, hygiene and children's safety in the kitchen, combined with sustainability (reduction of food waste), food justice and climate change concerning food production and consumption. Consequently, in this book we perceive Denmark as a laboratory for taste education.

The above-mentioned tendency is also apparent in other contexts than teaching and the food profession. As will be illustrated in this book, the perception of children, cooking, taste and well-being in society is generally far more inclusive than before. Here, too, focus is not only on nutrition and cooking skills but also on taste, well-being and social interaction with the so-called "competent child" (Juul 1995; cf. Part 1) as a focal point.

These tendencies should be considered in and supported through the teaching of the subjects that concern taste, food and cooking, and through other activities whose context builds on food and meals, food literacy and home economics as their educational objective. Therefore, the aim of this book is to qualify teachers and trainee teachers to teach, inform and communicate about taste in such a way that children and young people learn to make informed and conscious food choices based on knowledge and reflection on taste. One decisive precondition for this is the development of a systematic didactics of taste. That is the intention behind this book, which is a translation of *Smagens didaktik* (*Didactics of Taste*) (Wistoft and Qvortrup 2018a), however with a number of changes and modifications.

*

The book consists of three parts: a historical, a systematic and a didactic part.

Part One is a historical overview of children, taste and cooking from 1971 to 2016. This part goes over every cookbook for children published in Denmark in the period and shows that a radical change has taken place in terms of adults' expectations of what a child is: whereas the child in the 1970s was seen as an incompetent child in a dangerous and difficult kitchen, it is now a child that conquers the kitchen and kicks out the parents. The current trend has replaced the traditional focus on nutrition and accuracy with a focus on taste and creativity. Briefly speaking, "Home Economics" is turning to taste. Part two presents a system of taste with seven dimensions of taste, based and substantiated on didactic reflection. Part three is a didactics of taste, or, rather, a taste didactic reflection theory that offers a foundation for reflections on teaching about, through and for taste.

The historical part analyses Danish children's cookbooks from 1971 to 2016 with the aim of identifying the development in the view of children, cooking and taste. Slightly simplified, this part presents an answer to the question of 'when': when did the view of the kitchen change from something that was dangerous for children to something that was exciting and fascinating; when did the view of children change from incompetent and helpless to competent, independent and creative; and, not least, when did the view of taste change from a norm that was met by following a recipe as accurately as possible to a sense and ability that everyone, including children, possesses and uses as a basis for cooking and enjoying food, and develops in order to become taste competent, confident and autonomous?

Further, the historical part will demonstrate how the perception of what children are capable of has changed radically. We know this because we have read every children's cookbook published in Denmark from the entire period, 435 in total. In the 1970s, children were seen as incompetent and the kitchen as a dangerous and challenging place. The adults needed to protect and help the child. Via a development that we have followed in ten-year phases, the child today, according to the cookbooks, has become highly competent in the kitchen. Children rule the kitchens while adults are bustled outside to wait expectantly for the competent children to produce various delicacies. Today, kitchen behavior is not guided by health concerns and concise recipes but by taste and pleasure, and children are just as competent as adults, if not even more, in that respect.

This also means that the cookbooks have changed, and with them the didactics of taste. In the 1970s, the admonishing index finger was ever-present: 'beware', 'measure', 'tidy up'. The cookbooks focused on risk management, practical skills, health and nutrition. Cookbooks of the 2010s place unconditional faith in the competent and creative children: 'get your parents out of the kitchen', 'listen to your taste', 'experiment'. Contemporary cookbooks focus on creativity, taste and pleasure.

As described, the historical overview of children's cookbooks looks at the history of children through a magnifying glass; however, it is also a platform for the two following parts: one focusing on a system of taste, and one focusing on a didactics of taste. This book takes the view of children and Food Knowledge of the 2010s as its point of departure, which entails taste as a focal point. The aim is to develop and propose a didactics of taste.

The second, systematic part presents a taste systematic basis for a didactics of taste. Put simply, it presents an answer to the question of 'what': what is being taught when teaching revolves around taste, and which dimensions constitute taste?

The background for this part is that when we eat, our taste is not only a question of sense i.e. the sense of taste. We also eat in aesthetic, moral-political, health-aware and love-oriented ways, and we may eat with awareness of religious faith or of style. Does the food taste sour, sweet, salty, bitter or umami? Does it taste good or bad? Does the food leave a 'good' taste in the mouth, i.e. is it socially and ecologically sustainable? Does it taste healthy or unhealthy? Does it have a particular taste because the meal is associated with faith? Does it taste trendy, like we experience in a 'street kitchen' surrounded by friends?

This part identifies seven dimensions of taste: pleasant taste, healthy taste, sensed taste, moral taste, religious taste, loving taste and trendy taste. All these dimensions of taste are described with concepts taken from systems theory: characterized by a binary code, a symbolically generalized medium and a reflective basis. Further, they are interconnected through structural links. If this sound abstract and complex, Part Two demonstrates that the concepts are useful in understanding what happens when we taste, and it provides concrete examples of what the concepts mean.

The systematic part is introduced with a section called "Systems Theory Basis", which explains and substantiates the starting point in systems theory. This is followed by seven short sections on each of the dimensions of taste. All these include didactic reflections and concrete examples.

The third, didactic, part presents—again, put simply—the answer to the question of 'how': how can we teach about, through and for taste? The aim of the teaching is not only to present theories on the five basic flavors and knowledge on what is healthy and unhealthy or on producing and seasoning food, even though these are obviously also important skills. The aim of teaching revolving around taste is to qualify teachers and trainee teachers to become capable, through teaching, information and communication, of teaching children and young people to make informed and taste reflected food choices.

The precondition for this is the development of a didactics of taste: a didactics that employs a focus on teaching, learning and competency development, and which reflects on the seven dimensions of taste and the forms of knowledge and argument connected to and communicated through the teaching. If the dimension of taste is pleasant, the associated form of knowledge is 'I experience' this when I taste. The form of argument is aesthetic. When the dimension of taste is healthy, the associated form of knowledge is 'I know' this about what I taste. The form of argument is health-professional. When the dimension of taste is moral, the associated form of knowledge is 'I believe' this about what I taste. The form of argument is normative.

For example, some people think that pork chops are delicious, while others think they taste bad or foul. However, claiming to 'know' that they are delicious is a misconception. We may 'know' that pork chops have some specific nutritional qualities and 'believe' that it is okay, or not, that they are produced industrially. But in terms of taste, we 'experience' how the chops cause pleasant or disagreeable taste. If the aim is to teach children and young people to make taste conscious food choices, it is important that they know which forms of knowledge and argument are relevant and productive in relation to a specific dimension of taste.

The didactic part is introduced with the sections "Taste as Such" and "From System of Taste to Didactics of Taste". In "Taste as Such," a number of theories of taste are presented, based on the assumption that behind the different forms or dimensions of taste, taste exists as a quality in itself. This is the precondition for moving from 'what' to 'how', i.e. from the systematization of taste to a didactics of taste. The section "Didactics" presents the basic didactic concepts: learning, teaching and competence (skills and knowledge). This is followed by two sections on forms of knowledge and forms of argument. The final section presents suggestions on how to formalize the seven dimensions of taste and the forms of knowledge and argument in teaching. It also presents examples and ideas on how to teach with a view to students developing their taste competence, authority and autonomy.

*

The three parts of the book are connected by an overarching concept that needs to be clarified from the outset: what is meant by 'taste'?

The word 'taste' is used with at least three meanings.

First, 'taste' is used in a philosophical and aesthetic sense, cf. the concept 'Geschmack' in the writings of the German philosopher Immanuel Kant (1724-1804). Kant writes that the principle of taste is the subjective principle of the sense of judgement per se (Kant, 1971 [1793], 202): the sense of judgement can be exercised on a logical basis, for example based on the laws of nature ('I know that when I let go of an object, it will fall to the ground'), but judgement can also be exercised on a subjective basis ('I think that the food tastes bad, the music sounds weird, the painting is banal, the spring fashion is dull, the view from the hill is disappointing'). This is 'taste' in the broadest sense: the ability to sense and reflect when we judge a phenomenon aesthetically.

Second, 'taste' is used as an aesthetic concept regarding sense and judgement in relation solely to food and cooking. When we taste a well-prepared meal or season food in the kitchen, we use all our physical senses and our sense of judgement to evaluate the taste and tastiness of the food. We see, smell, feel and evaluate the texture of the food, we taste it in our mouths, and, at the same time, we activate our memories of taste to recall previous taste experiences. We talk about the food with others and arrive at a common judgement. This is 'taste' in a narrower sense: the ability to sense and reflect when we taste and season food.

Thirdly, 'taste' is used as a concept regarding the sense, and use of the sense, that is located in the mouth and on the tongue with its approx. 9,000 taste buds. Here, the sense of taste is a specific sense alongside the other four senses: sight, hearing, smell and touch. When we use 'taste' to describe what happens when we taste the food, we are thinking of what happens when the receptors on the tongue transmit signals to the brain, which processes these signals. This is 'taste' in its narrowest sense: that which happens when food activates the taste buds.

The English language has a conceptual distinction between taste in the second and third meaning. Taste as the ability to taste and season food is covered by the word 'flavor', whereas the process that takes place in the mouth and on the tongue is covered by 'taste'. The Danish language, as well as other Western European languages, does not have words to cover this distinction.

This book employs the concept of taste in the second sense: to describe our ability to reflect and sense when we use all our senses and our aesthetic sense of judgement, individually or collectively, to taste and season food. Thus, strictly speaking, the title of this book could have been: "Teaching Flavor".

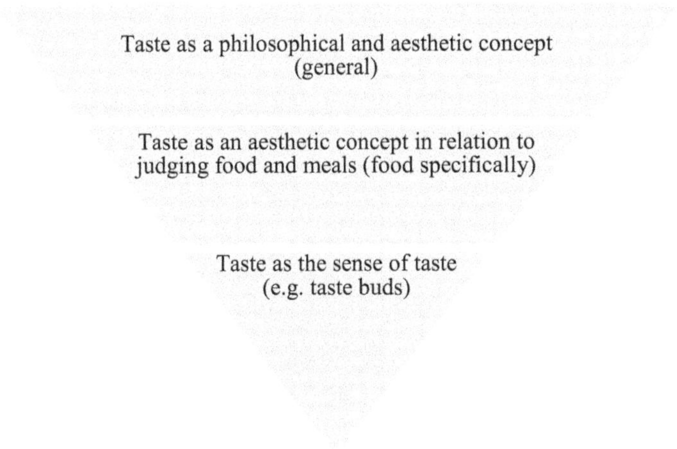

Taste as a philosophical and aesthetic concept
(general)

Taste as an aesthetic concept in relation to
judging food and meals (food specifically)

Taste as the sense of taste
(e.g. taste buds)

Figure 1: The three meanings of 'taste'

The target group for this book is teachers, trainee teachers and students on courses in Food Knowledge and/or Food Education. This includes teachers and students of Food Knowledge and Home Economics at teacher training colleges; teachers and students on professional BA courses dealing with food, taste, dissemination or didactics; teachers and students on MA courses dealing with food, taste, dissemination or didactics; teachers and students on dietician courses; and teachers and students on BA and MA courses dealing with food, taste, dissemination or didactics.

We hope this book will prove beneficial. We have certainly enjoyed and benefitted from writing it, and we would like to thank all our friends and colleagues who have contributed with professional input, good advice, comments and practical help with literature searches etc.

Thanks to our editors and reviewer for useful and constructive comments and suggestions. Thanks to Magnus Corvus and William Frost from Last Word Consultancy for thorough translation and proof reading. Thanks to lecturer in the History of Ideas at Danish School of Education (DPU), Aarhus University, Jens Erik Kristensen, for a thorough and constructive reading of the entire manuscript and for useful and precise comments. Thanks to lecturer in the Study of Religion, Aarhus University, Marianne Qvortrup Fibiger, and senior researcher at Danish Institute for International Studies (DIIS), Robin May Schott, for valuable input and comments on the section on religious taste. Thanks to Yoshihiro Murata, head chef at Ryotei Kikunoi in Kyoto, for input on the Japanese kitchen, and to the team at Agern (Grand Central Station, New York City) for inspiration on the section on pleasant taste. The authors, however, remain solely responsible for the finished result.

Karen Wistoft and Lars Qvortrup
Copenhagen, July 2019

PART ONE

Turning to Taste

In the Danish compulsory school, we have seen a turn in food education as well as Home Economics: from focusing on precision, nutrition and hygiene, the current focus is on taste, pleasure and creativity. This is not the result of a single person's or public department's intervention in the curriculum of Home Economics; rather, it is the result of a much broader process of social and cultural development, which includes a wide spectrum of changes, from the emergence of the New Nordic Kitchen, via changes in public food cultures, to a new perception of the kitchen, the child, and of upbringing and education in general. These processes have caused radical changes in Danish food education.

The common denominator for the emerging trend is that food education has changed from focusing on nutrition, precision and hygiene to focusing on taste, creativity and authenticity. The kitchen has become a site of pleasure and experimentation, rather than a dangerous place with sharp knives, boiling water and strict recipes, which have to be observed to the letter. Rather than being an insecure individual needing protection by adults, the child is seen as a competent person in their own right because the child's taste is as good as the adult's taste (Leer and Wistoft 2018). All these developments reflect the same elements that characterize the New Nordic Kitchen: authenticity, creativity and taste.

In order to support this argument, we borrowed and read every single children's cookbook published in Denmark during the period 1971-2016: not 10, not 100, but an astonishing total of 435 cookbooks, including books by Danish authors and books translated from other languages, but no reprints. Here, we can see the changes in the perception of children, kitchens, upbringing and food education, and we can see that nutrition gradually has been replaced by taste, precision by creativity, and hygiene by authenticity. It began modestly with a bit less than 40 children's cookbooks in the 1970s but then the number soared: between 2001 and 2010, around 180 children's cookbooks were published, or around 20 per year.

It is not only the large number of cookbooks that comes as a surprise. Even more surprising is the fact that this material shows that our perception of what a child is has changed over the course of this period of less than 50 years. In the 1970s, the kitchen was seen as a dangerous place to which defenseless and helpless children were only allowed access under supervision, subject to an array of warnings about the potential dangers of sharp knives and red-hot stoves, as well as various rules concerning hygiene. Today, by contrast, according to the cookbooks, children should have free access to the kitchen, and when the kids are cooking, parents are expected to wait patiently for the tempting results of their children's efforts to be presented and served.

Furthermore, cooking and kitchens are political arenas: the period since 1970 has witnessed several revolutions, beginning with the celebration of nutritional foods produced efficiently by the farming industry. Then came the health concept linked to the green revolution, later followed by the sustainability revolution favoring organic farming and animal welfare. This was followed by globalization and the multiethnic kitchen. Recently, gastronomy and Nordic cuisine have gained ground. Indeed, the food fight is a political struggle, also when children are the chefs.

In order to understand the interconnections between education and gastronomy, it is important to emphasize that Claus Meyer (for instance) is not just the co-founder of Noma and the main author of the *Nordic Kitchen Manifesto* from 2004 (Nordic Co-operation 2004; Leer 2016). He is also the co-author of one of the most influential children's cookbooks in Denmark, *Meyer's Kitchen Kids* from 2000 (Meyer and Poulsen 2000). Here, the focus changed radically from nutrition and precision to taste and pleasure. In 2013, the Nordic Kitchen Manifesto was supplemented by the Children's Nordic Kitchen Manifesto, emphasizing that "Every child in the Nordic countries has the right to learn to cook healthy and tasty food", and that "every child has the right to their own taste and to positive food experiences" (Nordic Council of Ministers 2014). It is obvious that the emergence of the New Nordic Kitchen is primarily a symbolic factor, although on the global stage it has appeared more glamorous than the 'modest' task of teaching taste to the kids.

EMPIRICAL BASIS: CHILDREN'S COOKBOOKS 1970-2016

The empirical basis of this part is cookbooks published in Danish during the period between 1970 and 2016. There are several reasons for choosing 1970 as the starting point. In a social context, 1970 is considered to be the starting decade of the modern welfare society with general prosperity, women entering the labor market and a new view on general education. In public schools, home economics changed from being a subject for girls only to also including boys. In a research context, a historical study from 2013 has identified all published cookbooks in Denmark from 1900-1970, including very few children's cookbooks (Nyvang 2013). The cookbooks included in our review study were written for children, although many of them addressed the parents (in other words, the parents were the recipients). The books were initially identified on the basis of their titles via the Danish Royal Library and were subsequently borrowed and read. The selection criteria were as follows: in order to qualify as books, publications had to be at least 16 pages long (in accordance with the definition used by Radio Denmark); in order to qualify as cookbooks, they had to contain recipes; and in order to be children's cookbooks, they had to contain recipes for children. A specific focus was on publications aimed at involving children in cooking.

Five-hundred-and-nine cookbooks were identified, 435 of which contained recipes for children. The remainder were books about food aimed at children and/or families, but written for parents, scout leaders, teaching assistants or others. Some textbooks, teachers' manuals and reprints were also omitted.

The children's cookbooks were categorized, and a data record was produced, containing photos of all book covers and notes on educational values and descriptions of taste in the books. The portfolio served as a reference work in the subsequent analysis. In the present article, books are only referred to with their titles translated into English. However, all the original Danish titles can be found in the reference list at the end of the book.

*

The first Danish cookbook for children was published long before the focus period. In 1847, the pseudonymous Madam Mangor self-published *Cookbook for Little Girls, Published by a Grandmother*. The little girls were brought up to become skilled and proper mothers and develop specific virtues that did not leave visitors in any doubt: "It is absolutely essential that the little girl not only maintains the hygiene but also makes sure that it shows in the food" (the quote is taken from an article from 2017 by Caroline Nyvang on Danish cookbooks from the 19th century). However, for many years, cookbooks for children were mainly intended to provide entertainment. They were used by the children of the upper classes when they played with toy stoves and doll's houses. It was the mother who reigned in the kitchen, and the other members of the family were expected to stand back, at least until the girls were old enough to be allowed access. And when they were, it was in order to be trained in the virtues and responsibilities of the housewife (Nyvang 2017).

Things did not really take off before World War II, and, as is the case in many other areas, it was probably the women's entry into the labor market that made the difference. Gradually, access to the kitchen was no longer an age and gender privilege: men and children were allowed in because the women had work to do elsewhere. A close study of each of the 435 Danish cookbooks for children published in the period 1971-2016 reveals a revolution in adults' views on children: from the small, non-competent children in the 1970s, who needed to be warned about the perils of kitchen life, to the competent children of our time who order their parents out of the kitchen, pay no heed if the food burns, and only call for their parents when it is time to eat. Reading cookbooks for children is like looking at the world of children through a magnifying glass: at the one end, we can zoom in on the small, helpless children in the kitchen; at the other end, the adults are kicked out of the kitchen by children who are more creative and independent than their parents.

Two comments should be added. First, most cookbooks for children are written by adults. So, what they demonstrate is not necessarily that the behavior of children changes, but that adults' views on and ideals about children change. Second, cookbooks for children are one basic element in a broader process. These cookbooks mirror changes in the view of the child, of education and upbringing, and of the ideals of food preparation and kitchen work. Thus, changes in child upbringing and food education are paralleled by changes in Danish food, kitchen and restaurant culture, which in the 1970s was still very traditional, but which experienced a radical change in the 2000s—a change that can be linked to similar changes in children's food education. Not until later was it possible to identify indirect causal relations: when new generations with a new food education background become adults, they enter the world of gastronomy with new skills, competences and expectations.

The Child as an Apprentice Chef

In the 1970s, the child was seen as an apprentice chef. The child was granted access to the dangerous universe of the kitchen under guidance and supervision. Most of the children's cookbooks from this period contain an introduction or a foreword addressed to the adults, and both adults and children are addressed in an admonishing tone: "In order to avoid accidents in the kitchen, it is important that children are thoroughly informed about the use of sharp knives, can openers, etc." (Söderqvist and Åberg 1971, 6), write Åke Söderqvist and Lasse Åberg in 1971 in the adults' introduction to *The Children's Cookbook*. Kirsten Brenøe's *The Children's Illustrated Cookbook* begins and ends with chapters named "Beware!" (Brenøe 1974, chapter 1), which provide vivid descriptions of both cutting and scalding accidents. The adults need to look after the children "because the kitchen is a very dangerous place to work" as stated in the adults' foreword (Brenøe 1974, 2).

The overall expectations of what children can manage are not very high: the point of departure is that the child is not competent. Herluf Petersen, in *We Are Cooking*, sets the bar so low that no one can be disappointed: "Even if we can't cook as well as mum, it's still fun to try" (Petersen 1973, 7).

Although the gender roles had not changed much, there was a realization in the 1970s that cooking was not only for girls: "It is a fact that many grown men cook, for instance if their wife is at work" (Petersen 1973, 7). However, apparently it is still women who have a knack for cooking, so if help is required, the reader is advised to seek "the guidance of mum or possibly granny" (Petersen 1973, 7), emphasizes Herluf Petersen, whose book also indicates that the green revolution had not reached Denmark: "Of course we can make everything easier by using canned goods" (Petersen 1973, 10). The same is noted by Söderqvist and Åberg: "In order to make our work easier, we have mainly used canned and frozen goods" (Söderqvist and Åberg 1971, 6).

The rhetoric concerning taste and the use of the concept of taste is also interesting. In this period, it is characteristic that the food is either not seasoned at all or only seasoned with a little salt. As apprentice chefs, the children should learn to cook, but the taste of the dishes is either irrelevant or a mechanical result of following a recipe, preferably to the letter. And as such, taste is not part of the cooking repertoire.

In the broader social arena, as long ago as 1962, a number of teenage milk bars, serving milk shakes with different flavors to young people, were established in Danish cities by the National Association of Danish Dairies. This was one of the first examples of a specific focus on young people's and children's taste. In 1972, the National Association of Danish Dairies published its first national cookbook, followed in the period 1980-2001 by eight cookbooks (*Caroline's Kitchen* 1-8), which were published every third year and distributed to all Danish households. In retrospect, this was an ambitious adult educational project, focusing in the early years on using milk, cream, butter and cheese, but also gradually introducing taste, globalization and creativity (Carlsen et al. 2008). There are two important elements in the process: the recognition of the child as an independent culinary actor, and the idea of educating people with the focus on their approach to food and cooking. A third element and a prerequisite for the New Nordic Kitchen is a recognition of gastronomy. In Denmark during the post-war period, the focus had been on health and nutrition, not on taste and pleasure. This also changed in the 1970s. In 1969, the old Danish inn Faldsled Kro [Faldsled Inn] was bought by the food entrepreneurs Sven and Lene Grønlykke. They invited the respected French chef Jean-Louis Lieffroy to Denmark, creating the very first gastronomic revolution in Denmark. In 1976, they founded Kong Hans Kælder [King Hans' Basement] in Copenhagen. In 1983, this was the first Danish restaurant to receive a Michelin star. But in general, Danish food culture was still oriented towards traditional values, with taste being regarded as an upper-class cultural phenomenon (Bourdieu 1979) supported by avant-garde artists.

The Child as an Assistant Chef

In the 1980s, the child was promoted to assistant chef. There is evidence of this promotion in *The Children's Cooking and Baking Book* from 1983: "You may think it's fun to help, but believe me, it's even more fun to do most stuff on your own" (Thomsen and Dørge 1983, 5). However, the children cannot be left completely in charge: "Have a chat with your mum about what you'd like to cook so she can explain how" (Thomsen and Dørge 1983, 5). The first edition of the book was published in 1969, and with its approximately 200 instructive recipes it is far more comprehensive than its counterparts on the market. The kitchen remains a place for girls: 68 of the many twee vignettes depict girls, whereas only 22 depict boys. Only in the section on cooking over open fire are the genders evenly represented.

There are lots of examples of children moving up in the kitchen hierarchy. In *Easy and Fun: Food for Youngsters* from 1982, Lene Hannestad notes that being able to cook makes a person less helpless, freer and more independent (Hannestad 1982). Similarly, teachers' manuals for home economics also emphasize that students need to acquire the tools to live independent lives (Pedersen and Birkum 1982).

This period also saw experiments with new forms of communication: it became standard to address the child directly, rather than through the adult. In Christina Björk and Lena Anderson's *Linus Cooks*, the authors address the reader at their level through the boy Linus. In this way, they also manage to sneak in the first political messages: Linus feels sorry for the battery hens and hopes the phenomenon will be made illegal (Anderson and Björk 1981). This strategy is also used in a different and much more effective manner in Walt Disney's *Donald Duck's Cookbook* from 1986, which contains the duck family's favorite dishes (Disney

1986). In a historical perspective, the book is in fact progressive because it focuses on good taste and completely avoids lecturing, preferring to address children on their own terms. The book was followed by *Mickey's Cookbook* (Disney 1987). Here, pleasant taste is also central, making the two Disney children's cookbooks distinctly different from earlier cookbooks with their imaginative descriptions of the taste of Donald's and Mickey's favorite dishes.

The green wave really took off in the 1980s. In 1984, Edel Broeng published *Green Food Healthy & Happy*. The author goes directly to the recipes, only emphasizing that "the knives have to be sharp" (Broeng 1984, inside cover no page number) because the vegetables will then be easier to cut. In 1986, Anne Vincents Nielsen and Kari Sønsthagen published *The Children's Green Cookbook*, another celebration of vegetarian food, which the children need to learn how to cook, both on weekdays and for festive occasions. The children need to know which vegetables are in season, and the book is bursting with useful green knowledge. The famous food pyramid is replaced with a vegetarian version, and the green knowledge is supplemented with knowledge about battery hens, so the children learn to distance themselves from the phenomenon (Nielsen and Sønsthagen 1986). The decade overflows with green cooking and fruit books, and already in 1983, a home economics leaflet was published on Food and Wild Plants (Stenkjær and Eskildsen 1983). So, anyone who thinks that foraging for dandelions and wild garlic is a phenomenon of the 2010s would be mistaken. In terms of taste, the green children's cookbooks do not provide specific taste descriptions. Anything green basically tastes good.

In the New Nordic Kitchen context, the 1980s provided two new elements. First, that food is political, not in a narrow but in a broad sense: following one's taste is part of a liberation process, and cooking is a political activity. Second, that one should resist the use of industrial products and rather turn to organic and/or vegetarian products. The New Nordic Kitchen could not have been realized without this popular tendency.

The Child as a Partner Chef

The next leap in the kitchen hierarchy took place in the 1990s, when the child became an equal partner chef. One of the most influential children's cookbooks from the period was Helle Brønnum Carlsen's *Yum: Love Until the Last Bite*, which was published in 1998 and was in reality a cookbook for adults containing children's recipes. Now it is the adults, rather than the children, who are being admonished: children's fussiness is a sign of common sense, which the adults need to respect (Carlsen 1998). Children's sense of taste must be taken seriously, discussed with the children and developed. In short: children are regarded as having taste competence, and meals are not just about nutrition and hygiene but also (equally importantly) about love and responsiveness. But children's taste also needs to be respected. In 1993, Kirsten Høeg-Larsen published the two books *Lasse and Lærke Cook* and *Lasse and Lærke Bake*, in which the children have become kitchen experts: "When there is pasta on the menu, Lasse and Lærke really look forward to it, because they have almost become experts at cooking pasta" (Høeg-Larsen 9). There are no adults to be seen in the many pictures of Lasse and Lærke: the children reign here, competent and self-assured. In 1994, the first book was published in which the recipes were developed by children for children and adults: Jytte Jensen's *Fantasy Bread: The Children's Best Baking Book* (Danmarks 4H 1994).

Furthermore, the role of the politics and morals of taste became increasingly evident in the 1990s. In 1990, one of Denmark's first celebrity chefs, Søren Gericke, published his *Children's Cookbook*, richly illustrated by the Danish artist Martin Bigum. In the book, the author addresses the children directly with clear, moral messages: "Be conscious" (Gericke 1990, 3). Food is not just something you wolf down. "Your choice could influence nature" (Gericke 1990, 3). Readers are expected to protect nature rather than devouring it, and are encouraged to ask shops: "Where do these radishes come from? Have they been sprayed?" because, as the headline points out: "You are what you eat" (Gericke 1990, 3). Camilla Plum strikes the same note with her book *Itsy, Bitsy, Meatball*, in which she blows the whistle on "functional food, alienation and anorexia" (Plum 1997, 7). In fact, her book is not a children's cookbook but a book for parents about cooking with children. Nevertheless, the message to the parents is that they should listen to their kids, because children are competent individuals in their own right: "Try and listen to what they want to cook themselves; their wishes usually reveal what they are able to manage" (Plum 1997, 11).

This tendency is even more obvious when comparing with the books that were translated from English in the same period. The view on children in Denmark was clearly different from that of the English-speaking world. Two cookbooks from 1991, translated from English, Angela Wilkes' *My First Cookbook* and *My First Party Book*, are full of warnings about the perils of the kitchen: Be careful with knives and ovens; remember to wash your hands (Wilkes 1991). The love of decoration which is apparent in these books, is an obvious contrast to the Danish celebration of authenticity and naturalness: decorate the ice cream to look like a bumblebee, and use potato chips and vegetables to make the dip look like a clown. The Danish cookbook authors from this period would never have written anything like that.

Finally, sweets and sugar were included in the list of positives, possibly because in the middle of the 1980s, scientific evidence suggested that sugar was not fattening. In 1993, Jørn Ussing Larsen published *Sweets for Little Sweet Teeth, Made from Pure Raw Goods*, which was followed by numerous children's cookbooks containing recipes for candy, desserts, puddings, cakes, etc. If only the children remembered to brush their teeth, sweets were both allowed and a hit (Larsen 1993).

This change in the way children in the kitchen were perceived in the 1990s was due to a radical change in the view of children and child upbringing. The popular-pedagogical milestone of the decade was a Danish bestseller on child upbringing published in 1995, written for parents and entitled *Your Competent Child* (Juul 1995). "Children who are treated with respect respond with respect" was the motto, and creating equality between the generations was a central ambition. This was also obvious in the kitchen. It was not possible to maintain the asymmetric distribution of roles between adults and children. On the contrary, the motto was that we are all competent, although in different ways, and that taste is the gateway to equality between different ages. Taste is an equalizer, because everybody (including children) has taste that must be respected by others. Thus, taste is perceived as a competence that cannot be transferred from one person to another. In order to develop taste competences, the child must be supported by a stimulating environment, e.g. in a creative kitchen.

This was also the case at the gastronomic level: by the mid-1990s, it was almost ten years since Kong Hans Kælder had received its first Michelin star. The achievement of a Michelin star was no longer a revolutionary event; it had become part of the gastronomic tradition. But during the 1990s, the realization came that taste and tradition are not interconnected. Good taste was not old taste but may be 'new'. Good taste was not French or Italian taste but had to be 'Nordic'. The stage was ready for the New Nordic Kitchen and a young generation of gastronomic entrepreneurs.

The Child as a Head Chef

In the 00s, the child assumed the position of head chef. This took place with instant effect from the beginning of the decade, when Claus Meyer and Ole Poulsen published *Meyer's Kitchen Kids* in 2000. The book starts with a genuine declaration of trust:

> We do not believe in the instructive qualities of even the most organic, purpose-driven meal situations. Nor do we believe in unconscious menu plans, devised with the dietician's clear sense of optimal nutritional concentration. We believe that in the long run, the joy of cooking and eating together is best developed when children experience that food is something that is prepared with a certain measure of gastronomic enthusiasm for the pleasure of oneself and others. We believe in the significance of challenging from the very beginning children's taste buds and stimulating their desire to explore the possibilities and mysteries of cooking (Meyer and Poulsen 2000, 4).

The trick was to wrench the kitchen out of the grasp of the adults' knowledge domains (organic farming, dietetics, menu planning, etc.) What counted were the possibilities and mysteries of cooking, which were closely related to taste and the exploration of taste—an area where everyone is equal: no one tastes more 'correctly' than others, and children are as much experts of taste as adults. In brief: taste creates enthusiasm and mental ownership, and it is democratic. It is probably no exaggeration to claim that this book and its insights were instrumental in changing the subject known as 'Home Economics' into 'Food Knowledge' in the Danish 2014 school reform, considering that the new subject prioritized food awareness, taste, and food and meal culture at the expense of nutrition, domestic skills, hygiene, and risk management. Among other things, Food Knowledge is a subject that focuses on taste, and anyone who can taste, argue for their taste and understand the different taste positions of other people meets all the requirements of the modern, reflective citizen. Basically, this means that the students learn to 'view' taste from various perspectives and, through this, learn to make informed and critical food choices.

The tendency to view taste as an essential factor triggered a new wave of children's cookbooks. Whereas about 35 children's cookbooks were published in the 1970s, almost 180 were published in the 00s, many of them with a focus on taste and pleasure. Heiberg's *Children's Dessert Circus* (Heiberg 2006) is made from plastic laminate to allow the children to taste, sense and experiment. "It is okay if you get egg on the book and butter on the pages, and it is okay if the worktop becomes a bit greasy" (Heiberg 2006, 9). One of the pieces of advice in the book (on chocolate icing) is: "Remember to lick the bowl well before putting it in the dishwasher" (Heiberg 2006, 13). Annette Søby, Ida-Marie Søby and Ester Larsen indicated with *Yippee, it's My Cooking Day* (Søby, Søby and Larsen 2006) that cooking was not an obligation anymore but a right and a celebration. The climax came with Katrine Klinken's *Cookbook for Princesses* (Klinken 2008). In this book, the democracy of food as well as taste and gender equality had developed to such an extent that it was okay (30 years after the focus period in this book began) to write a book aimed especially at girls. This is in total agreement with Heiberg: "Have fun with everything dreamlike, delicate and lovely and enjoy every single bit of the good stuff" (Heiberg 2006, 5). The underlying tendency was that we could no longer be bothered with the political correctness of the 1980s, especially because everything is about pleasure anyway.

In terms of cooking, taste and gastronomy, the 2000s truly presented a revolutionary time in which all the tendencies from the previous three decades converged into one major trend. It was a period combining the recognition of kids and teenagers from the 1970s; the understanding that taste, food and cooking are politics, and that it is important to use organic and/or vegetarian products from the 1980s; and the celebration of innovation and localism from the 1990s.

Obviously, this development and boom in children's cookbooks are not unique to the genre. They go hand in hand with the generally increasing interest in gastronomy and food culture. The restaurant Noma, spearheaded by René Redzepi, opened in 2003, received its first Michelin star in 2005, and the second in 2007. In 2004, 12 Nordic chefs drew up a manifesto for New Nordic Cuisine, establishing that not only the regional aspect but also taste were central to the art of cooking. The financial crisis may also have been a factor. The gastronomic boom happened before the crisis hit, i.e. riding the wave of financial surplus and optimism. However, the crisis also signaled that it was time to renounce globalism and superficiality at the expense of localism, authenticity and a down-to-earth attitude. Literally and figuratively, the time had come to forage for herbs for the soup pot, and family, children and community took center stage once again.

The Child as a Creative Chef

Since 2010, the child has become an independent kitchen creator. Not only have children become the bosses in their own kitchen, they are also creative forces because they are in close contact with their own taste and make their own unique dishes. *The Girlfriends' Cookbook* by Line Østergaard and Patrick Bachmann is a "declaration of love for your girlfriends and their cooking" (Østergaard and Bachmann 2016, 5). Instead of strict step-by-step recipes with detailed instructions, it is a tool for the reader to create her "own unique recipes". Pasta should be cooked until it "is as soft as you like it", and even though the book recommends that the reader uses 5 tbsp. of pesto, this is immediately modified: it "depends how much pesto taste you want" (Østergaard and Bachmann 2016, 14). It is important to use one's creative talents and create one's own recipes. At the same time, it is important to keep up appearances: "Use waterproof mascara when you dice onions, because they can easily make you cry" (Østergaard and Bachmann 2016, 11). Taste and pleasure are not only about food and cooking, but also about expressing the entire girls' universe.

The overall tendency is condensed in *MY Cookery* from 2014, published by the Danish Committee for Health Information with the chef Søren Ejlersen as the main author. A distinct feature of this children's cookbook is that the dishes have been selected by children from all over the country, after which eight celebrity child chefs have developed the recipes. *MY Cookery* begins with five tips on how children can get their parents to leave the kitchen: 1) Tell them how good you are; 2) Start simple; 3) Send them to get groceries; 4) Sing, especially if the food is burning; 5) Offer to clear up afterwards (Komiteen for sundhedsoplysning 2014, 10). The child has become a creative chef and therefore highly competent in terms of taste. Now it is time to create new flavors, serve and try them out in the company of friends and family, and adjust them. Taste is self-created, aesthetic, sensed and an expression of something social. Also, taste is something unique in nature, as it appears from the many recipes for cooking over open fire in *MY Cookery*.

As we emphasized in the introduction, what we know from studying children's cookbooks is that adults' view of children has changed. However, we do not know whether this has actually affected children's food practice. Are children's cookbooks not just another case of the wishful thinking of adults?

At least a little is known concerning the effects of one of the most influential cookbooks for children. As mentioned above, *MY Cookery* was published in 2014. In 2014-2016, more than 200,000 free copies were distributed to children in Denmark. In the second project period (2016-2019), it is expected that the same number of copies will be distributed, bringing the total number of copies distributed up to more than 400,000. The Danish Committee for Health Education, which is responsible for the distribution, has received a lot of feedback from schools, students and parents. Parents have indicated that *MY Cookery* has made them more aware of their own role in relation to inviting kids to enter the kitchen. Schools and teachers have responded that their students have been overwhelmingly enthusiastic about the cookbook. They have received the book as a 'gift' which they looked forward to taking home. They say that the book is of high quality, that it is inviting and elegant, and that the recipes are attractive for children. In addition, it is easy to access. These results are all taken from a research-based evaluation, which was led by Karen Wistoft and published in 2016 (Wistoft et al. 2016; Christensen et al. 2018).

The evaluation concludes that *MY Cookery* has inspired children and increased the pleasure of cooking for students in the new subject of home economics, both in schools and at home. The evaluation shows that

- *MY Cookery* has increased kids' inspiration and joy of cooking, both at school and at home.
- More than 60 percent of the kids answer that they cook more at home than they did before they received the book, and many ask their parents to leave the kitchen while they are cooking.
- They appreciate the visual presentations and the structure of the recipes, which implies that the children are more self-reliant in the kitchen.
- *MY Cookery* is used in home economics classes by 92 percent of the teachers who have answered the questionnaire (Wistoft et al. 2016; Christensen et al. 2018).

Consequently, even though only one cookbook for children has been systematically evaluated, this indicates that the view of children's competences, and of cooking as a creative and taste-oriented activity mastered by children, is not just wishful thinking, but that the book actually influences kids' cooking practices.

THE CONQUEST OF THE KITCHEN: UPBRINGING, EDUCATION AND GASTRONOMY

There are many potential stories to be written about children in kitchens between 1970 and today, all showing that a striking number of changes have taken place over this short period. For instance, children's cookbooks in Denmark document a development that began by disapproving of sugar and sweets, then celebrated sugar and deserts in the 1990s because sugar was considered harmless and almost healthy, but then with The Sugar Sheriff from 2009 once again disapproved of sugar and gave instructions on how it is possible to live a sweet life without sugar.

They also document globalization: in *The Children's Cooking and Baking Book* (Thomsen and Dørge 1983), the most exotic recipes, apart from 'tiger cake' and 'African milk', are pizza, spaghetti and macaroni. In 1987, the Danish Broadcasting Corporation published *The Kazoo Cookbook* (Nilsson 1987) with exciting fruit and vegetables from distant countries, foreign spices and pictures of children with various ethnic backgrounds. In 2007, the TV host Bubber recommended in Around the World in Denmark (Carlsen and Bubber 2007) that we taste the world with an open mind. But it is only in recent years that kitchen globalization has become a reality, in the sense that there is no longer a distinction between Danish and foreign dishes: in *MY Cookery*, bread rolls can be found side by side with naan bread, roast pork with avocado-tomato salsa, green bean salad with couscous salad, and open meatball sandwiches with pulled pork burgers.

The 435 children's cookbooks published in Denmark in the period 1971-2016 demonstrate that even though children are probably basically the same today as they were in the 1970s, our expectations of what they are, and what they should be capable of, have changed. The history of the children's cookbook is the story of the child, and the story of the child is the story of the adults' expectations of what a 'real' child is. The basic message is, however, that a revolution has taken place over less than 50 years: children used to be regarded as insecure and incompetent, needing their parents to guide them through the perils of kitchen life and sharp knives; now they are regarded as independent and competent, needing their parents to leave them alone in the kitchen. Cookbooks for children used to celebrate science and progress with nutritional instructions and detailed recipes, but now focus is on taste, the senses and creativity. This change has been paralleled by changes in the adult world of gastronomy in Denmark: from restaurants serving traditional dishes with very little innovation, through a phase inspired by French and Italian gastronomy, to today's celebration of innovation, authenticity and localism with taste as the important core of the New Nordic Kitchen.

*

It is evident that a revolution has taken place over less than 50 years. We have moved away from the idea of an insecure and incompetent child, guided through the risks of kitchens and sharp knives, towards a self-reliant and competent child who cannot wait to kick its parents out of the kitchen. From a world that revered science and progress with nutritional and dietary guidelines and concise recipes, to a world of taste, sensuousness and creativity.

In summary, the children's cookbooks also have many stories to tell. They are testimony to a development that initially disapproved of sugar but later on, in the 1990s, paid tribute to sweets and desserts because sugar was considered harmless, almost healthy, until *The Sugar Sheriff* in 2009 once again warned against sugar, providing strategies to reduce, or even ban, sugar intake (Foghsgaard & Lund, 2009). The same attitude is found in *Sugar Free Kids' Party* from 2015, which contains suggestions for a sweet and good time without any sugar (Ingemann, 2015).

The books also tell a story about globalization. In the *Children's Cooking and Baking Book*, the most exotic item, apart from a 'tiger cake' and 'African milk' (a term for chocolate milk that no one in their right mind would use today), pizza, spaghetti and macaroni (Thomsen & Dørge, 1983). In 1987, the Danish Broadcasting Corporation published *The Kazoo Cookbook* that features exotic fruits and vegetables from distant places, foreign spices and pictures of children with various ethnic backgrounds (Nilsson, 1987). In 2007, the Danish children's TV personality Bubber recommended in *Around the Globe in Denmark* that we taste the world with an open mind (Carlsen & Henriksen, 2007). However, it is only in recent years that kitchen globalization has become a reality in the sense that there is no distinction between Danish and foreign dishes. There is also more focus on global flavors now, as well as on pleasant, healthy, sensed and 'trendy' taste.

In conclusion, many stories could be written about children in kitchens from 1970 until today, all of which would prove that immense changes have taken place over this short period. They also prove that even though children are probably not that different today compared to the 1970s, our expectations of who they are and what they are capable of have changed. The history of children's cookbooks is the history of the child and of what adults expect a 'real' child to be.

The transformed view of children has been accompanied by changing expectations for what children should learn and how they should approach taste in the kitchen. To summarize:

In the 1970s, taste was not on the agenda. Recipes were followed to the letter and creativity was limited to the optional pinch of salt at the end. Here, the recipe and, obviously, the adult author, was the authority and the child a novice meant to follow the recipe. In the 1980s came the advent of green and healthy taste, making taste something to talk about. Still, there was no reason to consider taste and flavor because anything green was healthy and hence good by default. The same was the case in the 1990s, when moral and political taste entered the stage: battery hens tasted bad whereas free-range, 'happy' hens tasted good. Taste was moralized and politicized, but the authority on taste was still situated outside the individual child. Surprisingly, though, this was also the decade when sweet taste was liberated, the big leap happening in the 2000s, when sensed taste and pleasure took center stage. When it came to sensing and enjoying, we were all authorities. It is possible that adults and children have different opinions, but we all have a right to our opinion as long as we can substantiate it. The trend of the 2000s was extended and intensified in the 2010s, when children are not only taste and kitchen authorities in their own right but also have the opportunity to express their taste-based competences creatively.

The child of the 2010s is a modern, tasting and creative child whose creativity and pleasure are fundamental. The present book is written with this child in mind, addressing the question of how we can educate children to become competent, taste-oriented kitchen authorities. The suggested approach is to give them a vast number of skills, but also to contribute to their ability to make reflected judgements of taste based on the seven dimensions of taste that we have introduced and will expand on below: first, in Part Two, which focuses on a system of taste; and, subsequently, in Part Three, which investigates how children can be taught to develop practical and reflective taste competences.

As already said, many stories could be written about children in the kitchens from 1970 until today. However, the main story is the story of taste. Over the course of less than 50 years, the focus of food education, Home Economics, as well as the general view of children, food and kitchens have changed: From nutrition, precision and hygiene to creativity, pleasure and taste. With a focus on taste, children move to the center, because taste is democratic. We all have our own taste. With a focus on taste, kitchen work becomes creative, because taste is something that we have to experiment with instead of strictly following a recipe. In brief: over less than 50 years, we have experienced a turn to taste.

As mentioned above, we do not find the same development in other countries (Leer and Wistoft 2015; Wistoft and Qvortrup 2018b). In recent years, in the international research arena concerning food education and/or home economics education, there has been an increasing focus on nutritional science, hygiene, health science and education towards sustainable development (ESD). However, with the emerging changes in the view of children's competencies and the authenticity of their taste experiences, combined with an increasing measure of gastronomic enthusiasm for the pleasure of taste and the importance of the meal community (Meyer and Poulsen 2000), we have experienced an increasing interest in the didactics of taste. This book is written to accommodate this interest.

PART TWO

A System of Taste

Teaching that revolves around taste entails two fundamental questions. One concerns the object of teaching: what is taste? The other concerns the approach to teaching about the object: how can we teach taste? At the same time, it is important to stress that the two questions are not completely separable. The way in which we define and describe the object of study depends on what we want to use the definition for. There is a difference between defining a phenomenon scientifically and didactically: a scientific definition and description must live up to scientific criteria and be unambiguous and exhaustive; a didactic definition must describe the teaching subject and its aims, the framework, teaching content and learning objectives in order for them to be communicated and realized in a manner that is educationally beneficial. The following definition and systematization of the phenomenon of 'taste' is developed in a didactic perspective.

This brings us back to the question: what is taste in a didactic perspective? Is it something to do with pleasure, whether individual, i.e. having taste experience as individuals, or collective, i.e. enjoying the meal in the company of others? Is it a physiological phenomenon that focuses on taste buds and sense impressions and expressions? Is it about health and taste education contributing to children acquiring a taste for healthy rather than unhealthy foods? Or is taste a moral phenomenon that regards a taste for the good and responsible life, based on awareness of moral issues and on choosing foods that are produced with a view to sustainability and acceptable production environments?

Our answer is that taste encompasses a number of dimensions. How many there are can only be decided empirically. In this book, we have included seven dimensions, but it is an open discussion whether there are more. It is also a valid point that all seven dimensions may not be equally important. Regardless of how many there are, didactics of taste can be defined as a theory on how to teach taste in a way to ensure that students acquire knowledge and skills regarding all relevant—in this case, seven—dimensions of taste.

Let us begin with an illustrative example. A family is staying in a holiday home, gathered around the table to eat the freshly-caught plaice they have brought home from a stall by the harbor. The plaice is served with freshly dug potatoes and homemade sauce, and everyone uses their senses to see, smell and taste the food, feel it in their mouths and hear the sounds of chewing the crispy, battered surface of the fish. They judge the taste combinations and impressions, and activate their aesthetic repertoire and memories of taste. They enjoy reminding each other about having bought the potatoes at a local, organic farm, which makes the food taste even better. They are pleased that the meal 'feels' good at the same time as being healthy, and that they have taken time to prepare it and to enjoy it together. Is the careful preparation not an entire declaration of love that makes the food even more pleasant? Sometimes there is an almost religious dimension to the experience: there can be something otherworldly about the opportunity to experience a meal community. And, finally, the entire meal might be orchestrated in accordance with the TV food show that the family watched just before leaving for the holiday home, where there was an episode on how celebrities spend their summer holidays.

In brief, there are many dimensions of taste at play in an ordinary meal, and the example above identified seven dimensions: 1) we taste aesthetically and think that the meal is delicious; 2) we taste in relation to health and are pleased that the food is healthy and that we have time for each other in connection with the meal; 3) we use our sense of sight, hearing, smell, touch and taste, i.e. the entire sensory repertoire; 4) we discuss organic farming and sustainability when we conclude with pleasure that the vegetables taste good because they are organic and produced locally; 5) we activate the religious taste, thinking that the meal is heavenly; 6) we clearly sense that the food is prepared with love and experience the taste of a loving meal; 7) and we agree that by serving and eating food in this way, we are trendy, i.e. we identify as 'foodies'.

Figure 2: A system of taste

However, if we are to relate systematically to taste and its dimensions, it is not enough to describe it in an unstructured way through everyday concepts. That goes for all professions. If a layperson describes a disease, they use everyday concepts: 'The patient seems feverish and feels unwell.' But a doctor uses health professional concepts and a systematic approach. The same applies to any form of didactics, including didactics of taste. It is necessary to develop a systematic set of concepts or categories to draw up a precise description of the subject. Here, we are inspired by the sociological systems theory as it was developed by the German sociologist Niklas Luhmann (1927-1998) from the 1970s onwards. Not because Luhmann was an analyst of taste, but because we believe that his concepts are useful in the present context. We have also noted that Luhmann himself chose his sources of inspiration for developing adequate concepts rather freely. For example, he took some of his key concepts from biology and 'translated' them into social science. In principle, we do the same: we take a set of concepts from sociological systems theory and translate them into a theory of taste.

This second part of the book is introduced by a section that explains and substantiates the central concepts from systems theory used in the book. This is followed by seven short sections on each of the seven dimensions of taste. All these contain didactic reflections and examples, some of which are taken from the 435 children's cookbooks reviewed and analyzed in part one, while others are taken from the school subject of Food Knowledge as well as other contexts. As emphasized above, what we present in this book is not a scientific system of taste; it is a subject-oriented, didactic system of taste.

SYSTEMS THEORY BASIS

A system of taste is a systematic overview of the dimensions of taste. In other words, it is an overview of which dimensions are included when we taste something and when we talk with others, i.e. communicate about what we taste.

But before the overview of the dimensions of taste, a foundation is needed, i.e. a system of concepts that are common to all dimensions of taste, whether they refer to aesthetic taste, healthy taste or moral taste. This is no different to other subject areas. Architects use the same basic concepts whether they talk about villas, skyscrapers or extensions. The same goes for those of us who talk about taste.

The German systems theory sociologist Niklas Luhmann has already been mentioned as a source of inspiration for this system of concepts. We are aware that his concepts are sociological and ours concern taste. However, as mentioned above, Luhmann also took concepts from other subject areas and transferred them to sociological theory, e.g. the concept of 'autopoiesis' from the Chilean biologists Varela and Maturana's theory on how biological systems function: they are closed systems that recreate themselves on the basis of themselves. The same, claimed Luhmann, goes for social systems.

Secondly, we talk about taste as a social phenomenon. When individuals taste something, they have their own individual experience. But if we share our experience with others, for example in a shared meal, we obviously need to make our experiences communicable, or we have no chance of understanding what others experience when they taste something. This is why the system of taste is a sociological system. It concerns how we communicate about taste.

The following part will go over the basic concepts: binary code, symbolically generalized medium, reflection repertoire and structural links.

Binary code: the first assumption is that in order for taste experiences to be communicable, they must be describable in a sociologically recognized code (Luhmann 2000 [1984]). If I hurt myself, and I want to tell others that it hurts, we have to agree on communicating in a code that makes it possible to distinguish: does it hurt, yes or no? Once that code, which is a binary code because it distinguishes between a plus and a minus, i.e. a yes or a no, has been established, it becomes possible to differentiate within the scale of the code: does it hurt a lot or a little? Anyone who has been in hospital knows that it is common to hear the questions: Does it hurt? How much on a scale from one to ten?

The same applies in the case of communicating taste: does this taste good? In order to answer, it is necessary to distinguish between pleasant taste and the opposite, bad/ disagreeable taste. It is described as a 'plus or minus deliciousness': +/- delicious. The same goes for the other dimensions of taste: does it taste healthy, i.e. +/- health? Does it taste of love, i.e. +/- loving taste? etc. It is possible to define grades within all these binary codes: the freshly picked strawberries are not just good or bad, they might be amazing, rather good, rather plain, slightly watery or really bad. Regardless of judgement, however, the starting point is a plus/minus scale based on a consensus. The strawberries may also taste good or sustainable, they may burst with love or be seasoned with balsamic vinegar, rather than cream, to taste trendy.

Symbolically generalized medium: this brings us to the next concept, the 'symbolically generalized medium'. Obviously, it is not possible to use a binary code without knowing what it is a binary code for. Are we talking about pleasant taste, healthy taste or trendy taste? As early as 1979, Niklas Luhmann wrote a book about power, in which he emphasized that 'power' is not a concept of action but of communication, related to defining who has the power to do what. For instance, the senate has the power to pass a bill if the majority is in favor, whereas the president cannot force through a bill: he or she cannot force others to accept it but will have to use their persuasive powers to make the senate support the bill. This means that it is crucial to make clear whether communication takes place through the symbolically generalized medium of 'power' or 'force' (Luhmann, 1988).

This also applies to taste: are we communicating about pleasant taste, healthy taste or trendy taste? In order to distinguish between the three, we need to use a symbol, i.e. a sign, for the phenomenon in question, and we need to be able to generalize that symbol. For example, when is something a chair, and when is it a sofa? The answer is that it depends on whether the object is suited for one or several people. A symbolic generalization has taken place.

Symbolically generalized communication media use symbolic generalizations to communicate. If the topic of communication is pleasant taste, the communication criterion is: does the food taste good or bad?

If the topic of communication is healthy taste, we judge whether it tastes healthy or unhealthy. But does the healthy not always taste good? No: anyone who has given broccoli or spinach to their child knows that children will sometimes cringe or turn their noses up, followed by the well-meaning parental comment: 'try to eat it, it's healthy!'

Reflection repertoire: when we communicate about taste and various other things, we use a binary code that represents the plus and minus value of a symbolically generalized medium. But when we argue through a symbolically generalized medium, we need to be able to relate to it. When someone says, 'this strawberry tastes wonderful', they should be able to account for what it means when something tastes wonderful. They should be able to answer the question: 'what do you mean by that?'

In order to answer, the person has to draw on a reflection repertoire, i.e. a 'stock' of knowledge that supports reflections and provides words for the distinctions they make. For example, we may substantiate the difference between agreeable and disagreeable taste by referring to and making use of an aesthetics of taste that offers reasons for why something is agreeable or disagreeable. The reflection repertoire also provides the possibility and criteria for discussing the distinctions we make. One person may argue on the basis of aesthetics of taste— how and why something appears to taste different to different people. Or we may discuss what role it plays for the taste experience that our eggs come from free-range chickens. In this case, the reflection repertoire is ethics, i.e. arguments regarding whether it is more or less morally correct to eat eggs produced in one manner than another.

Structural links: how are the seven dimensions of taste interrelated? They might appear hierarchically ordered; first, we sense the food and then we judge it in terms of pleasure (aesthetically), health and/ or morals; finally, we decide whether there is faith, love and/ or style connected to the taste. However, it is our opinion that the dimensions of taste are of equal weight and interdependent. We cannot sense without experiencing agreeable or disagreeable taste, just like we cannot experience agreeable taste without sensing the taste of the food. With yet another concept from systems theory, we could say that they are structurally interlinked. Actually, in his systems theory, Luhmann uses the concept "structural couplings", but in this book we prefer the more common concept "structural links" (e.g. Luhmann 2012 and 2013). The argument is that the seven dimensions of taste are all operatively closed: they refer to each their reflection repertoire and operate in each their code. A person who is only interested in pleasant taste will find it difficult to understand that animal welfare should also be taken into account: 'this salmon is tasty, and it doesn't influence the taste whether it was stressed when it was caught.' At the same time, the dimensions of taste do not exist independently of one another. Most people would probably be willing to admit that if the animal they eat has had a miserable life, it influences the taste experience negatively. We express this as the different dimensions of taste providing 'structures' to each other: the healthy taste uses structures from the sensed taste, e.g. from the five basic flavors, to express in what way something tastes healthy or unhealthy. Accordingly, pleasant taste may use references, i.e. structures, from the repertoire of ethical taste. 'Organic pork chops are more delicious than chops from conventionally produced pigs', we might say, without always being able to substantiate it within a narrowly defined taste aesthetic dimension: we use ethical concepts to support an aesthetic statement.

However, we also use the concept of 'structural links' in other connections. Biological phenomena, for instance, are structurally linked to mental phenomena, i.e. the individual taste experience, which, in turn, is structurally linked to social communication when the individual accounts for their experience. Electrical signals are released via receptors and transmitted to the brain, where they are structurally linked to the consciousness, i.e. the mental system, and thereby the sensed taste becomes consciousness; this, in turn, is linked structurally to the communication system via language, causing the individual taste experience to become available to a social community. However, we all know that this is not a frictionless process: we can sense and taste something that it is difficult to express communicatively, partly because sense experiences are pre-lingual. Therefore, language has to provide a structure that ensures our ability to link sense experiences to social communication.

Finally, this overview of concepts needs to decide whether the phenomenon of 'taste' always exists in the form of dimensions of taste. Our answer is that in order to discuss whether taste has different dimensions, i.e. different forms, we have to accept the precondition that the phenomenon of 'taste' exists 'in itself'.

The point of departure for the system of taste is, therefore, that we can talk about or imagine that taste exists 'as such', i.e. as a quality in itself. But does taste exist 'in itself'? The German philosopher Immanuel Kant would answer affirmatively. Beyond the way in which things appear to us as phenomena, they exist 'in themselves' (Kant, 2002 [1787]), i.e. before they are given form. Niklas Luhmann would distinguish between distinctions and the blind spot of distinctions, i.e. between what is being sensed and the position from which it is being sensed. As the Danish philosopher Ole Thyssen writes in his book *The Wonder of Recognition: A Little Book about Observation*, we cannot see the latter position ourselves (Thyssen, 2004, cf. also von Foerster, 1984)[1]. Accordingly, we distinguish between taste as such, i.e. as a pure quality, and forms of taste. As long as taste appears as a pure quality, it cannot be observed, i.e. sensed and described. That can only take place when taste is given form via one or more of the seven dimensions of taste.

Luhmann used light as an example on several occasions: we cannot see light as such; it is a pure medium in terms of observations of sight. But if the light creates shadow, we can see it indirectly, and we can see it if it shines through a glass prism, where it creates a color spectrum, or when it shines through a stained-glass windows. In these cases, light is given form as a medium for other observations, which makes it observable. It is our contention that the same applies to taste: taste

---

[1] As everywhere in this book, Danish book titles have been translated into English. The original Danish title can be found in the list of references.

as such cannot be observed, but we can observe taste when it assumes form, whether it be sensory, aesthetic, moral, health-related or whichever of the seven dimensions of taste it appears through.

Each of the seven dimensions of taste will be described below, while an outline of 'taste as such' can be found in the opening section of Part 3. The seven dimensions of taste are summarized in the below table: each dimension is characterized by a specific binary code; communication about the dimension of taste in question takes place within a symbolically generalized medium; communication and substantiated judgements of taste take place on the basis of a reflection repertoire, i.e. comprehensive common knowledge about the dimension of taste. Each part of the table will be elaborated below.

Table 1: Dimension of taste, symbolically generalized medium and reflection repertoire.

Dimension of taste	Symbolically generalized medium	Reflection repertoire
Pleasant taste	Pleasure	Aesthetics, incl. gastronomy
Healthy taste	Well-being and nutrition	Knowledge about health, incl. nutritional science
Sensed taste	Sensory perception	Knowledge about sensory perception, incl. sensory science
Moral taste	Social norms	Ethics, incl. food ethics
Religious taste	Faith	Knowledge about faith, incl. religious food and meal rituals
Loving taste	Love/passion	Knowledge about love articulated through food/meals
Trendy taste	Style	Knowledge about fashion and style expressed through food/meals

PLEASANT TASTE

Dimension of taste	Code	Symbolically generalized medium	Reflection repertoire
Pleasant taste	+/- delicious	Pleasure	Aesthetics, incl. gastronomy

As mentioned in Part One on the history of children's cookbooks, Claus Meyer and Ole Poulsen published *Meyer's Kitchen Children* in 2000. The declaration of intent believes that in the long run, the desire to cook and spend time around the table is developed when children in a community experience that food is something they prepare with gastronomic enthusiasm, for the pleasure of themselves and that of others. The aim is to challenge children's taste competencies and taste autonomy early, and to stimulate their desire to explore the opportunities and mysteries of cooking on their own. The dimension of taste promoted here is the one whose dominant code is +/- delicious. Does the food cause pleasure or displeasure? In the book, Meyer reminisces about 1992 when he launched 'The National Day of Taste', which at that time was met with a lot of skepticism. Back then, children were not supposed to taste the food while cooking, and they had to follow the exact recipe. But his book introduced a new era of taste and sensuousness as crucial preconditions for cooking. In Denmark, this tendency was continued in 2001 when Meyer and Poulsen published *Sweet Stuff*, in which they recommend tasting, smelling and stuffing oneself with fruit to experience the juiciness of life (Meyer & Poulsen, 2001). In 2002, the same authors published *Favorite Packed Lunches*, providing ideas for making packed lunches that will make the children hear "angels sing" (Meyer & Poulsen, 2002).

It is obvious that the symbolically generalized medium in Meyer & Poulsen's books is pleasure. The children are expected to savor 'sensuousness' and 'stuff' themselves with fruit; in short, they are expected to hone their ability to taste in a way that not only entails tasting whether something is sour, sweet, salty, bitter or umami, but also the ability to substantiate what tastes delicious and why. This means that the basis for reflection is aesthetic: more specifically, the aesthetic of taste. From having been guided by health, nutrition or morals, the didactics of taste is steered in an aesthetic direction. The pleasure-oriented didactics of taste aims to contribute to the student's ability to substantiate their pleasure, i.e. that something tastes delicious. The student should be able to express an aesthetic judgement of taste.

It is also obvious that pleasant taste is structurally linked to other dimensions of taste: that something is tasty seems to imply that it is also healthy and morally beneficial. Likewise, substantiating why something tastes delicious or not involves structures from the sensed taste: it tastes good because it has the right level of sourness, sweetness or saltiness.

According to Kant, the aesthetic judgement of taste is, in contrast to other judgements, indeterminate. Delicious taste cannot be proved or unequivocally defined. It is individual and self-reliant. 'I don't like lasagna' can be—and is—substantiated tautologically: 'I don't like it because I don't like it'.

Nevertheless, both in general life and in teaching, we look for substantiation and aesthetic judgement. If good or bad taste is to be substantiated, it initially has to happen through association. This or that taste is 'reminiscent' of something, i.e. the taste of Christmas pudding is reminiscent of candles, pine needles and oranges. Subsequently, however, it happens socially, because that which cannot be substantiated externally has to be substantiated through communication with others. The consequence is that delicious taste and the criteria and substantiation for delicious taste must be found in the social community. The social has two dimensions: the horizontal (contemporary community) and the vertical (the past-present dimension). The horizontal dimension is for instance found in meal communities, where judgements of taste are exchanged and discussed. Taste experiences are shared and substantiated around the table, often with reference to social traditions. In one culture, crispy pork crackling is delicious, whereas in another, pork is abominable. It is important that the students learn that this is the case. The vertical dimension is, for instance, found in memories of taste, i.e. the agreeable or disagreeable taste created over time. The memory of taste plays a big role; the taste of a warm kidney pie is substantiated in the memory of warm kidney pie, and the mere sight of a specific taste object evokes a repertoire of memories of taste.

The development of pleasant taste and the aesthetic taste experience is particularly evident in modern gastronomy, which can be perceived as a kind of laboratory for refinement of the sense of taste and for making well-founded judgements of taste. The process may stem from expensive restaurants but has spread to a wide section of society. In the first decade of the 2000s, wild herbs and other ingredients were something reserved for especially advanced restaurants, but only a few years after the trend started, ordinary supermarkets had wild garlic and sea buckthorn on their shelves.

One of these laboratories is found in the Danish-owned restaurant Agern, located in Grand Central Station in New York City. From the beautifully restored modernist station, it is possible to step into a gastronomic 'den', whose shape and color refer to the name Agern (acorn). It is a change of scene, so to speak, from the pulsating station to a space that focuses on calm, peace and aesthetic beauty. The menu is based on farmed and wild produce from the New York State region, prepared and served in accordance with the principles of New Nordic cuisine. When we visited the restaurant, there were two tasting menus: 'Land & Sea' and 'Field & Forest'. The first included land produce, such as tomatoes, beetroots and bee pollen, combined with seaweed, fish and shellfish. The latter included potatoes, cabbage, onions, mushrooms, honey, apple cider, nuts, goat cheese, etc.: everything that can be found in forest areas and in the fields surrounding forests. The beverages played a special role; there was no traditional wine menu, but instead a combination of beer, aquavit, water and different wines. The concept of 'non-alcoholic pairing' stood out: amazing beverages were produced, mixed and shaken on site, often based on the same ingredients as the menu.

Initially, the dishes merely tasted pleasant because they were good, i.e. substantiated in themselves and stimulated by the magical ambience in the restaurant. Subsequently, associations started to unfurl because the meal was built around a narrative about land, garden, field, forest and sea, i.e. about provincial life and authenticity substantiated in the Nordic cuisine. Finally, the experience became a foundation for social interaction around the table, with chefs and waiters as participants and contributors in the background: we tasted the food, associated to other experiences and discussed the ingredients, the food and the presentation. In other words, we created a confident community of taste. We tasted. We used our senses. We gave our opinion and listened to that of others. We tested the validity of our and others' taste arguments. In brief, we practiced being part of a community of opinion based on taste.

Delicious and disgusting taste are substantiated in the aesthetic reflection repertoire as it is, e.g., systematized in taste systems such as gastronomy, i.e. knowledge about pleasant taste. The word comes from the Old Greek *gastros* ('stomach') and nomos ('rule' or 'law'). A particularly significant example of aesthetic communities of taste is wine tasting. Immediately, the individual participant likes or does not like a specific wine, but then the discussion gets going about immediate taste preferences. The initial arguments are associative: a particular taste 'is reminiscent of' freshly-cut hay, wet grass or chalky soil. Subsequently, the participants systematize their arguments by ticking off taste forms, the results of which are tallied and converted into scores. This is a good example of how a community of taste is created in wine tasting (the horizontal dimension of the community), where memories and expectations of taste (the vertical dimension of the community) are included. An instructive example of the associative reflection on taste is provided by the Danish anthropologist Susanne Højlund in her book on taste, where she quotes a newspaper food critic's description of a taste experience: "Quiet, facetted and still insistently vegetarian, with the bitter perfume of fine crème and a hint of deep sweetness from deep-fried reindeer moss. Aristocratic elegance with contempt for vulgar culture" (Højlund, 2016: 27).

Our conclusion is that while pleasure and displeasure are semantic opposites, building on emotional terminology, it is difficult to pinpoint the exact opposite of disgust. Also, viewing pleasure and displeasure on a continuum is problematic, because it may assume that both pleasure and displeasure cannot be experienced at the same time. One example is that while chili pepper in a dish may cause pain to some people, others might believe that this element of displeasure adds an extra layer of depth to the food, contributing to its pleasantness.

The taste didactic consequence is that the student should be able to substantiate their taste experience on an aesthetic basis. The starting point is that something tastes good or bad 'because'. The next step is to search for associations, i.e. discuss what a certain taste is reminiscent of. The third step is to become part of a reflecting taste community and substantiate taste in memories of taste. Finally, we can add a fourth step: understanding that taste is formed in taste cultures and social taste regimes that experience taste very differently and connect social identity with taste. This may result in reflective taste tolerance, which is an important element of a modern, globalized society.

Teaching Example: Pleasant Taste

The students can work with substantiating taste experiences on an aesthetic basis. What does it mean that something tastes delicious or unpleasant, and how does it manifest itself in the taste? They can work with what a certain taste reminds them of, i.e. with memories of taste: in which connection can they remember something that tasted especially good or bad? They can work with food and meal cultures, where taste is experienced differently. Why is it that we think something tastes good at specific times, in specific situations and with specific people (family, friends, etc.)?

Meat or no meat?

Whereas a traditional European/North American meal includes meat as a central element and potatoes, pasta, and/or rice as secondary elements, accompanied by vegetables and possibly a sauce, a vegetarian meal is composed differently, as a series of dishes cover nutritional requirements in combination and provide pleasant taste and fullness. The students can prepare a vegetarian menu and a meat-based menu and compare their aesthetic qualities: how does the food taste, what do they prefer, and why? What is delicious, and why?

Locally or industrially produced?

Industrialization and development have had a strong impact on the global food market. Focus on longevity, hygiene and standardization is still dominant in many of the ready or semi-ready meals we know today, but the growing interest in local produce and cuisine puts emphasis on 'labor' and appreciates local and seasonal variety. The students can prepare dishes based on the two paradigms (local/global) with a focus on discussing tastiness and reflecting on the advantages, disadvantages and aesthetic qualities in that relation. What is tasty food in our local area compared with the global? What does it mean that food is 'local', and how can we say that food provides specific aesthetic qualities?

The students can search for relevant information and reflect critically on a given food source by searching the Internet or reading relevant books/ leaflets from institutions such as the Agriculture and Food Council or producers who publish relevant background material. Emphasis should be on pleasant taste in connection with the information at hand. The students can 'taste' the pleasant taste in the various written documents and try recipes and instructions with the aim of discussing pleasant taste in relation to local or national recipes.

HEALTHY TASTE

Dimension of taste	Code	Symbolically generalized medium	Reflection repertoire
Healthy taste	+/- Health	Well-being and nutrition	Knowledge about health, incl. nutritional science

A good example of teaching taste through the reflection repertoire of knowledge about health is the school subject of food education or Home Economics. Here, a distinction is made between a broad health concept in a well-being perspective and a health concept with a view to nutrition and the healthy body. It is the broad health concept that is the foundation for the subject of food education. A broad health concept entails both living conditions and lifestyle (Wistoft, 2009). A view to well-being entails a focus on personal resources and social values such as mental health (Wistoft, 2012). A view to nutrition entails a focus on how food influences the healthy body (Krogager & Olsen, 2010). Healthy taste signifies how food and meals are judged in regard to well-being and nutrition. Healthy taste is especially relevant in relation to discussions and reflections on healthy food choices. Food education as well as Home Economics are subjects in which the students have the opportunity to collaborate and socialize around food and meals. A conscious effort is put into working with how joy of life, well-being, health and taste must all be considered when qualifying food and meal choices.

Health in a Well-being Perspective

Well-being is linked to personal involvement and social food and meal values. If meal communities are built on joy of life, equality and social responsibility, they can contribute to furthering social well-being. Well-being signifies a comfortable feeling that entails energy, drive, resolve and pleasure in cooking and eating with others. Well-being was originally linked to a holistic health concept that expressed both the individual's subjective experience and the opinion of the surroundings (Wistoft, 2012). Here, the concept of well-being can be linked to the students' own judgement of the meals and other social factors in relation to their peers and networks (including digital). In that respect, it is important that it is the students' own judgements that are used to evaluate the degree of well-being.

A health concept with a view to well-being can apply different perspectives, resulting in slightly varying perceptions of healthy taste:

a) The students' general development in relation to food and health

b) The students' perception of meal communities

c)   The students' understanding and expectations regarding food and health

d)   The social interplay in relation to food and meals

e)   The students' influence on, and active participation in, cooking and meal communities

Healthy taste in a well-being perspective is, therefore, about the students' own experiences, expectations and assessments of the opportunities for considering health through taste in food and meals. In other words, there is a strong cultural link between healthy taste and pleasant taste. It is clear that a positive expectation of being able to change taste, food and consumption has an effect on health promotion and well-being, because the ability to influence taste in itself influences health and well-being. Healthy taste is optimized in constructive interplay between expectations and self-evaluation, and taste education must accommodate these by establishing real possibilities and spaces to act and gain knowledge about the connection between health, taste and well-being.

In practice, this can be ensured by teaching the students to cook healthy food (this is elaborated below), giving them the opportunity to serve the food for others, so that they can be proud of it, and leaving them enough time to eat together in a relaxed and cozy atmosphere.

Health in a Nutrition Perspective

Another aspect of the reflection repertoire for healthy taste is related to the nutritional health concept. If we stick to the example of food education or Home Economics in school, knowledge and skills in relation to nutrition and food are also evident when it comes to healthy taste. In Food Knowledge classes, students work with nutrition on the basis of the three main sources of energy: protein, fat and carbohydrates, in connection with groups of food, which makes the sources easier to recognize in their everyday forms. This is done, for example, through small experiments where the students search for carbohydrates in foods, both in theory and practice, or make a catalogue of different types of fat according to the connection between firmness and saturation. Teaching can also focus on vitamins and minerals, directing attention to the students' acquisition of concepts and theoretically structured knowledge about the healthy body, alongside a focus on how they can transfer this knowledge to their daily life. This aspect of the reflection repertoire relates to nutritional science: for example, theories on energy demand compared to intake; acquisition of knowledge about proteins, fat and carbohydrates, vitamins and minerals; and energy demand and balance. The students focus on vitamins and minerals, on professional terms and how to use them in practice. The teaching content is typically structured in the following three categories: a) digestion and factors influencing the energy demand; b) the impact of carbohydrates, fats, proteins, fibers, vitamins and minerals on health; c) the content of energy, energy-providing nutrients, fiber and significant content of vitamins and minerals in foods.

The focus is on digestion and energy demand, the impact of energy-providing nutrients and fibers on the body, and the content of them in different foods. Teaching also entails vitamins and minerals and their function in the body. Nutrition and energy demand can be treated as an independent theme. Energy-supplying nutrients and fibers can be exemplified by means of relevant foods and by experimenting with them. If the theme is fats, lists or exhibits can be made of different types of oil and fat, and butter can be produced from high-fat cream. Proteins can be exemplified by producing cheese or gluten, or by experimenting with fish. Also, nutrition and energy demand can be linked to teaching diets and food awareness. For example, the nutritional importance of polyunsaturated n-3 fatty acids and vitamin D can be reflected in connection with fish.

Different diets are typically linked to nutritional health. The concept of 'diet' is not unambiguous but is often used when a nutritional perspective is applied to food/ drink and meals. Dietary recommendations regarding cooking and meal composition are typically based on various health and nutrition considerations. In that sense, diet is judged on at least two levels: 1) the food level, by means of dietary models and recommendations; 2) the nutritional level, by means of diet programs in which the nutritional contents of food are calculated and assessed in light of common nutrition guidelines. The important thing here is that the teaching should include intentional learning objectives that are linked to dietary recommendations, dietary advice and models, and that assessments are made at the nutrient level (limited to the content and distribution of energy and level of fiber). The arguments for this are both learning-related and professional. Partly, they reduce the level of complexity for the students, and partly they contain the key message: overeating and an unbalanced distribution of the energy-providing nutrients, carbohydrates, fat and protein, are the main reasons behind dietary diseases today (obesity, type 2 diabetes, etc.)

Taste education in a nutritional perspective thus employs a health concept based on the healthy body, where health is seen as a result of what we eat compared to what we burn, with a focus on the balance between intake and use (BMI, Body Mass Index). However, it is important to mention that the concept of a 'healthy body' is perceived differently and can vary across cultures. This BMI concept of health concentrates on nutrients in food, which—like the health concept in a well-being perspective—facilitates different teaching focuses: the students' assessments of health based on knowledge about nutrition and energy demand; the students' assessments of health messages, diets, dietary recommendations, etc.; and their options in regard to furthering nutritional health, e.g. through preparing their own food and meals.

Compared with pleasant taste and pleasure, which are judged in terms of aesthetics, healthy taste must be judged in terms of knowledge about healthy food or healthy meal communities. As described in the previous section (page 22), aesthetically substantiated taste is not 'worse' than healthy taste; it just represents another dimension of taste. Healthy taste is judged on arguments for healthy versus unhealthy food and healthy versus unhealthy meals. Healthy taste is identified in opposition to unhealthy food.

Also, there are evident examples of structural links between healthy taste and other dimensions of taste. For example, healthy taste can be linked to moral taste in the case in which vegetarian food is considered not only to be sustainable and thus morally qualified but also to be healthy. Similarly, when parents prepare packed lunches with lots of nicely prepared vegetables, healthy taste is coupled with loving taste. As a third example, healthy food trends such as kale in the United States, e.g. *10 Health Benefits of Kale* (Gunnars 2018) and several other parts of the world, or cold, freshly pressed fruit and vegetable juices, are considered to be smart, thus representing the trendy taste. It is often said that healthy food tastes better than unhealthy food, sometimes based on an almost 'Rousseauian' idea of children being in closer contact with what is natural than adults, enabling them to choose healthy foods without being prompted. Organically grown carrots simply 'are' more delicious than the conventionally grown. Hereby, the ethics and political ideals of taste or aesthetics provide a structure, e.g. in the form of a language, to health – and vice versa.

The students can work with these structural links by tasting, reflecting on and comparing healthy and unhealthy foods and discussing whether there is a connection between health and tastiness, and what constitutes this possible connection. Do healthy foods in fact taste better, or is it simply nice to know that the food is healthy? Can we taste that the meal is more than food and full stomachs? Can we add to the healthy taste of the meal through increased pleasure, wellbeing and sense of community?

Teaching Example: Healthy Food and Carbohydrates

This brief example aims to illustrate some general thoughts related to healthy food when presented during lessons in the subject of Home Economics in primary and lower secondary school. The students can work with three of the four competency areas: Food and Health, Food Awareness, Foods and Cooking. The overall objectives are:

- The students can account for carbohydrates as a source of energy and nutrition and their connection to taste

- The students can identify carbohydrates in foods on the basis of categorizations

- The students can carry out an investigation of the significance of carbohydrates for taste in cooking

- The students can bake 'home-made' bread from flour that is particular rich in carbohydrates

- The students can analyze the significance of carbohydrates for health and well-being.

The teaching is built on an understanding of the concept of carbohydrates. Through small practical experiments with exemplary foods: fruit, greens and cereals, the students link the concepts from the theoretical teaching to practice. The requirement for different carbohydrates, and how to recognize them in practice (sweet carbohydrates are short-chained, etc.), is analyzed. The students work in an experimental and creative way with the carbohydrate-rich foods to interpret healthy taste. For example, they may develop bread recipes, work with yeast-based dough or make sauces. This will develop their understanding of the food-chemical effect of starch in different types of yeast-based dough (basic principles for the best wholegrain bread), flour-thickened sauces (difference between wheat flour, corn starch and potato starch) and similar products (the function of Béchamel sauce in homemade versus industrially produced lasagna). The students' own food products can be analyzed in regard to nutritional value, meal value and overall taste value. A major food-chemical effect of making bread dough also involves protein (i.e. gluten). As gluten is a controversial topic in the area of nutrition and healthy food, it might be used as an interesting teaching topic for students.

SENSED TASTE

Dimension of taste	Code	Symbolically generalized medium	Reflection repertoire
Sensed taste	+/- Sense experience	Sensory perception	Knowledge about sensory perception, incl. sensory science

When we talk about sensed taste, we are dealing with a dimension of taste that leads the didactics in a sensory and physical/chemical direction. In other words, sensed taste regards the sense of taste, i.e. the complex connections between the biological taste buds, the associated biochemical processes and the psychological sense experiences. Thus, the matter concerns culinary sensory science (Andersen, 2013) in which the sense of taste is central.

Sensed taste is explained by natural science: in the membranes of the taste cells, there are different receptors that are sensitive to the five different basic flavors: sour, sweet, salty, bitter and umami (Mouritsen & Styrbæk, 2015). Currently, many researchers are studying the notion of basic tastes, Research is quite controversial regarding how many basic tastes there are, and evidence for more than five basic tastes is hotly debated. For example, three suggestions for other basic flavors are fatty taste, strong or spicy taste, and astringent taste. The suggestion of fatty taste as a basic flavor is discussed by Eva Ryman (Ryman, 2015), strong taste is discussed by Mouritsen and Styrbæk (Mouritsen & Styrbæk,

2015), while astringent taste is discussed by e.g. Shepherd (Shepherd, 2011) and Mouritsen and Styrbæk (Mouritsen & Styrbæk, 2017). The conclusion, however, is that none of these three suggestions can be defined as basic tastes.

When the flavors are recognized by and bound to the receptors, an electric signal is released via a number of biochemical processes and transmitted to the brainstem and on the brain (Mouritsen & Styrbæk, 2015: 34). However, it should be stressed that the sensed taste, as seen from a natural scientific perspective, cannot be reduced to this description because it will always be a result of an integrated, multisensory process in the brain that encompasses chemical taste, smell, mouthfeel, sight and hearing (Mouritsen & Styrbæk, 2015: 32). Further, it is also important that it does not make sense to perceive the experience of taste as merely a sensory-physiological phenomenon. It also always has a social, psychological and cultural dimension that is connected to norms, education, life style, aesthetics, values and identity. In this sense, the approach includes the same broad and differentiated concept of taste that this book systematizes in seven dimensions.

In the dimension of 'sensed taste', taste is seen as a sense phenomenon that communicates impressions processed in the brain. New research continually provides insights into the capability of receptors and nerve pathways, and how the response to an impression can cause a specific taste. But even though the reflection theories are developed, this does not apply to the understanding of taste. In brief, research operates with a biological body where some molecules exist and are registered by a sensory apparatus, which transmits the signal to the brain. This leads to a process in which the brain links the response on the sensory impressions to cognitive levels.

Different natural scientific disciplines deal specifically with the sense of taste, utilizing knowledge from the various disciplines. Below is a list of five of the approaches that dominate the field (compare with the three meanings of the concept of taste presented in the introduction, pp. 12-14). The five approaches have been presented in the book Towards a Pedagogy of Taste: A critical literature review about children, taste and learning (Leer & Wistoft, 2015):

A. Flavor alone in the sense of what is sensed directly on the tongue and in the mouth, where it is perceived as a chemical-physiological phenomenon that is mainly located in the approx. 9000 taste buds (Mouritsen & Styrbæk, 2015).

B. Flavor in a sensory-physiological sense, where it is perceived as an integrated, multisensory process that involves chemical taste, smell, mouthfeel, sight and hearing. Here, flavor is a result of evolution and complex interaction between macro sensors. It includes a broader range of brain functions than any other human activity (Shepherd, 2011). In other words, this regards the impact of different sensory impressions on flavor and the interplay between the individual sensory impressions. The point is that all five senses are involved when we taste (Khandelia & Mouritsen,

2012). The Danish gastro-physician Ole Mouritsen is particularly interested in mouthfeel, which includes chemical or mechanical reactions that are not part of the primary mouth sensation. Here, it is not the five basic flavors that are central, but chemical or mechanical reactions or links to receptors on the tongue (Mouritsen, 2015, 2016). Chemesthesis, associated with a burning sensation, and astringency describe the sensitivity of the skin and mucous membranes towards chemical impact that causes irritation, pain or damage to cells and tissue. Both are mechanical effects on the mucous membranes (Mouritsen, 2016).

C. Flavor in a neurological sense, where it is the result of the 'image' that appears in the brain when we taste. In English, 'flavor' describes the total amount of taste impressions, whereas other languages do not have the same distinction. All components of 'flavor' utilize cranial nerves to communicate with the brain. Mouritsen describes how especially three cranial nerves: the olfactory nerve, the optic nerve and the so-called fifth nerve, play a central role in this transmission of flavor. He also describes how, typically, neurology of taste is concerned with flavor as a physical-chemical phenomenon but also, and in particular, the impact of smell and mouthfeel on the sense impression (Mouritsen, 2014).

D. Flavor in neurogastronomy, which draws on the above taste-neurological insight that flavor is created in the brain. Here, flavor is seen in connection with emotions, memories, language, learning, consciousness and, hence, food preferences (Shepherd, 2011); thus, flavor becomes important in terms of why we like the food we like (Prescott, 2012). Here, neurogastromy forms a scientific basis for gastronomy.

E. Flavor in gastro-physics, where it is seen broadly as something that results from the chemical composition of ingredients, biochemical processes and physical characteristics (Mouritsen, 2016). Combined with knowledge, taste impressions and memories, the broad concept of flavor in gastro-physics represents an approach to learning that Ole Mouritsen, among others, has practiced in his effort to integrate gastronomy and gastro-physics in order to create interest in, and motivation for, learning about the physical and chemical aspects of food among children and young people (Mouritsen, 2014).

Sensed taste is reflected on the basis of one of these five approaches. The point is that they all take their starting point in the same natural scientific (sensory) concept of taste.

Teaching Example: Sensed Taste in Connection with Cooking

The above five approaches to sensed taste can be transferred to taste education. Once again, the school subject of food education or Home Economics can be used to exemplify how. Here, the area of cooking can be described under the headlines of: Structure and Aims of Cooking; Basic Methods and Food Technique; Physics and Chemistry of Cooking; Taste and Seasoning; and, Aesthetics of Food. The syllabus is an example of structural links between sensed taste and pleasant taste. Here, however, we focus on sensed taste in cooking and seasoning (Lunding & Nielsen, 2011). Basic Methods and Food Technique focuses on students' knowledge of boiling, frying, baking and thickening, and subdivisions of these and techniques such as peeling, slicing, chopping, whisking, kneading and deboning. Within this area, students can work with different basic methods and techniques of preparing food and dishes. This is closely connected to sensed taste and choice or development of recipes, and to the aim and structure of the meal. The students can practice basic methods of cooking and preparation, i.e. boiling, frying, thickening, baking, grinding and preserving, which helps them build practical skills and authority. They need to know about the different basic methods and tastes, and about which techniques and combinations are suited for specific foods and dishes.

Seasoning can be central, and it may be important that the students acquire knowledge about the basic tastes, sour, sweet, salty, bitter and umami, and what smell, texture, astringency and irritation (burning mouth sensation) mean in terms of taste experience. The students need to develop a professional terminology for sensed taste, smell and texture. They can be trained in seasoning and expressing taste in words. They can work with describing texture, aroma and the five basic flavors, initially in isolation and subsequently in food combinations. They can investigate what combinations of different tastes or textures can bring to a meal, and how to use combinations of taste. They can work with experiments, recording and blind tasting, and subsequently use their experience to season their food. They can also work with the taste of spices and herbs that cause irritation, e.g. black pepper, chili and horse radish, or peppermint, which causes a cooling sensation in the mouth. The students can be presented with the taste of different local and foreign ingredients. It is important for the students' learning that they process sensed taste through words and concepts to stimulate awareness about the underlying sensory knowledge and understanding in order to push the boundaries of ingrained taste preferences.

MORAL TASTE

Dimension of taste	Code	Symbolically generalized medium	Reflection repertoire
Moral taste	+/- Moral accept	Social norms	Ethics, incl. food ethics

The dimensions of taste described up to this point are pleasant, healthy and sensed taste, and the associated reflection repertoires are aesthetic, health professional and sensory. The first repertoire, the aesthetic, is dramaturgic and distinguishes between pleasure and displeasure or delicious vs. not delicious taste, while the following two distinguish between known and unknown and whether they are declared 'true' in a health professional or sensory view. We feel that something tastes delicious or disgusting, but we know (or believe we know) whether something is healthy or unhealthy, or whether it tastes sour or salty.

A fourth 'regime' within judgements of taste is moral. Here, we distinguish between what is right and wrong. It tastes 'right' to eat sustainable products, whereas it leaves us with a 'bad' taste in our mouth to eat foods produced under environmentally unacceptable conditions. Eggs are a good example: should we make our omelet from cheap, conventionally produced eggs or choose the ones from free-range chickens? It is hard to tell whether our family will be able to taste the difference, but surely eggs from chickens who have roamed around in a field will give a better 'gut feeling' and therefore better taste? The example shows how pleasure and disgust are structurally linked, i.e. provide linguistic arguments for the moral of taste. Or, as Kant expresses it: taste can cultivate morals (Kant, 1971[1793]).

Moral taste is formalized as taste norms, i.e. as categorizations of what is right and wrong in a taste perspective. These taste norms are the results of general social norms, which therefore function as the symbolically generalized media of this dimension of taste. Over the last twenty to thirty years, there has been an increase in the amount of organic and unsprayed vegetables in supermarkets, and most of us know which products are best to put in our shopping carts. The same tendency can be traced in children's cookbooks: the last decades have seen a growing number of organic cookbooks, bursting with norms for taste, e.g. *Caterpillar Track Goodies* (Nielsen, 2012), where children are taught that saving money is environmentally friendly. Picking and preserving berries is good: it ensures that we know what we are eating. The reader is invited into the author's universe, where food waste is a no-go, and second-hand clothes are trendy. The author even calls herself a 'second-hand goddess' (Nielsen, 2012). A similar example is found in the children's cookbook published by the Danish Hunters' Association in 2015, *Wild Food in*

School: hunting for good ingredients, in which the students can follow game from hunt to table. Game contains no additives and hardly any fat, and, according to the book, for that reason simply tastes better than farmed meat (Nielsen & Holmberg, 2015). It is also evident that the development of taste norms has resulted in further differentiation of taste categories. Not many years ago, the only distinction between eggs was between big and small. Today, we distinguish between many kinds of egg, including cage eggs, eggs from free-range and organic chickens and barn eggs or eggs from local farmers.

The taste norms can, in turn, form the basis of binding decisions in the form of taste policy, i.e. politically binding decisions on what we can and cannot eat, or what is imposed with high or low taxes. In European countries and North America states, taste politics are primarily linked structurally to health policy: alcohol, cigarettes and sugar-rich products are tax liable. In other countries, 'gastro-national' taste is also rewarded, e.g. in South Korea, where 'the Korean cow' is protected by practically banning the import of beef. Another example is France, where all schools work one week a year with 'La semaine du goût'. Here, the students learn to distinguish between French gastronomy and, for example, ketchup, burgers and other types of foreign food (Leer & Wistoft, 2015; see also Chevrier, 2011; Garnier, 2001; Puisais & Pierre, 1987).

Finally, the students need to know about the reflection repertoire of moral food: ethics. Just like aesthetics can be defined as the knowledge mobilized when we reflect on our initial judgements of taste, ethics can be defined as the knowledge used to reflect on moral judgements. When using moral taste, we can, for instance, spontaneously say that the mere sight of foie gras makes our stomach churn, maybe because the image and description of force feeding, propagated by animal rights groups, pop up in our mind as the seared fatty liver is served:

> Foie gras is fatty liver, produced by force feeding ducks and geese directly into the stomach through a long plastic tube. Food is pumped into the stomach of the bird through a funnel or by use of compressed air. Due to the force feeding, the bird develops an abnormally fatty liver, 6-10 times larger than a normal liver. Force feeding in the production of foie gras is extremely stressful and painful, causing much suffering for the birds (Animal Protection Denmark, 2017).

But why is that so bad, and what consequences does it have for other things we eat? Here, the students have to consider their arguments, i.e. reflect on the moral judgement. In other words, activate their taste ethical repertoire.

Teaching Example: When and Why are Certain Foods Ethically Acceptable?

As a concrete example, the class could read texts published by animal welfare/rights organizations and compare them with texts from gastronomic media etc. For example, Animal Protection Denmark write:

> We are fighting for more natural food production and a sustainable food culture, focusing on quality, thoughtfulness and respect for animals and nature. Our ambition is for the entire food production in Denmark to be changed to either free-range or organic, and for Danes to reduce their consumption of meat, eggs and dairy.

This is based on the following argument:

> Danish food production is driven by a one-sided focus on growth, economy and low costs. Today, 99 % of all farming is intensive, large-scale production with dire consequences for animal welfare. Animals are treated as production units, not as living beings. This means that millions of animals in Denmark are living under highly criticizable conditions (Animal Protection Denmark, 2017).

But is trying to increase productivity and reduce costs really so bad? How did agriculture look a hundred years ago, with its limited, mixed production, no inorganic fertilizer and wide-spread use of labor? It may have been more pleasant, but both the living standard and average life expectancy were lower. What would happen to the national economy if the entire food production changed to free-range or organic, and how would it affect the global supply of food if everyone thought and acted in accordance with these standards? Whereas moral taste denotes that a specific food tastes morally right or wrong, ethics of taste reflects on why this is the case. It is important to ensure that the students take part in this type of discussion.

In addition, there are structural links between, for example, moral and pleasant taste. Does foie gras taste so morally bad that it affects potential tastiness? The website gastromand.dk presents an almost exemplary structural link: foie gras is "a bone of contention among many gourmands: can you handle the taste of bad conscience?" This question is followed by a series of recipes using foie gras (Gastromand, 2017).

When the two Danish chef brothers James and Adam Price in 2010 presented a recipe for foie gras on one of their TV shows, they tried to do so in the same way that they present any other recipe (Price, 2010). However, they did not get away with it; immediately after the show, an animal protection organization made a public complaint, and the case was covered in a newspaper on June 1st 2010, where the brothers were given an opportunity to defend their decision:

> In the cookbook published in connection with the TV show, we discuss foie gras, concluding that it is an individual decision whether one's gastronomic enthusiasm for foie gras outweighs one's reservations towards the production aspect. We have made up our minds, which is why we use foie gras (Politiken, 2010).

The Price brothers chose what below is termed the individualized moral approach to the topic, pointing out that it makes more sense to turn the attention to animal welfare in other and more wide-scale areas such as the production of chickens.

However, this was not the end of the story. The discussion flared up again in 2014, sparked by a TV show about the production of foie gras, which prompted the animal rights organization Anima to contact the brothers. Subsequently, Anima could proudly proclaim:

> Anima has entered into dialogue with the Price brothers about the tragic conditions under which the ducks live, and we have received the following positive statement: 'Foie gras will no longer be served in our restaurants, nor will we promote foie gras on TV as long as the ethics can be questioned' (Anima 2014).

At the opposite end of the spectrum, we find an article by the web editorial team on the Danish newspaper Information: "The animal rights organization Animal Friends has published a list on their website of restaurants and supermarket chains that sell foie gras" states the introduction, adding that this provides a list that comes in handy for gourmands searching for this exquisite viand. It is not easy to locate; few places sell it and it is perceived as expensive and exclusive.

From the moral level for or against foie gras, the article moves on to ethical reflection and argumentation:

> [T]he fact is that there is no end to the hypocrisy when it comes to arguments in the debate about animals and humans. Foie gras plays an utterly insignificant role in the sales figures of supermarkets Fundamental to the relationship between animals and humans has always been, and is still, that humans use animals for our own benefit, from pigs to fish, from food to shoes. This is based on consensus (Information 2000).

Moral taste also has a natural place in taste education, including Food Knowledge. The students should be able to reflect morally on taste and food. They should be able to relate to the structural link between moral and pleasant taste, i.e. between ethics and aesthetics: can food produced under unacceptable conditions still cause pleasant taste, or can we, so to speak, 'taste' the moral deficiency? They should learn that taste norms are socially founded, as expressed, for example, through the fact that they change over time; moreover, they should understand that food policy is founded in political decisions that provide justification for binding taste norms in society. Currently, we do not like certain foods because we perceive them as morally wrong. They can be banned or subject to varying degrees of taxation. As Animal Protection Denmark conclude in their critique of foie gras: "We recommend that you never buy foie gras or order it at a restaurant because the production is completely unacceptable in any respect." This comes with a recommendation to the Danish parliament: "Ban foie gras" (Animal Protection Denmark, 2017). As shown, moral judgements can be translated into political decisions, both at the individual level, i.e. encouraging individual action, and the collective level, i.e. encouraging binding political decisions. The student should learn to analyze and reflect on moral judgements according to a case as the above.

RELIGIOUS TASTE

Dimension of taste	Code	Symbolically generalized medium	Reflection repertoire
Religious taste	Immanence/ transcendence	Faith	Knowledge about faith, incl. religious food and meal rituals

Niklas Luhmann introduces his book on religion of society (in English, it is called "a systems theory of religion"), *Die Religion der Gesellschaft*, with the question: "How does one identify certain social appearances as religion?" (Luhmann, 2000a: 7, our translation). He answers: "We can say that communication is always religious when it looks at immanence through a lens of transcendence" (Luhmann, 2000a: 77). Translated into more common, action-theoretical sociology, we might say that it is not possible to decide whether something is religious on the basis of social practice alone. Certain social practices may come across as religious to some, while to others they merely constitute collective habit. One example is Easter lunch. For Christian people, it is part of the celebration of Christ's resurrection. They go to church in Easter to hear about the resurrection and then they go home and celebrate it with a ritual meal. For others, Easter lunch is merely an opportunity to make a gastronomic effort, which is why it can be served on any day during the Easter period.

In other words, to paraphrase Luhmann's words, how can we identify a certain meal or a culinary experience as religious? The answer is that we know this when the meal or experience as a social phenomenon is viewed in a divine perspective. If a meal is characterized as divine or heavenly, or if it is intended to make something divine or heavenly concrete and present, it is about religion. If a dish is divine, or if the entire meal makes us feel lifted from our profane daily lives into a transcendent reality, such as the Danish author Karen Blixen's *Babette* did with her feast (Blixen, 1958), it is a manifestation of religious taste.

However, other sociologists associate the phenomenon of 'religion' with ritual practice. They would say that certain social occurrences are about religion when they take place in accordance with certain ritual structures. One of the founding fathers behind this view is the French sociologist Émile Durkheim (1858-1917). According to him, religion can be perceived as a manmade system of symbols, rituals and religious ideas that build on a division of everyday life into holy and profane (Durkheim, 1915). As a sociologist, Durkheim saw this division as a result of the societal need to create social coherence. A specific religion is a collective system of religious ideas and habits that are substantiated in something outside society that is defined as holy, and therefore not to be disputed or discussed, and which unites everyone who conforms to these ideas and habits in a religious or moral community. Such a community can be a congregation, a religious denomination or a church, and the habits and ideas can form the basis of a regional, national or international community. Here, religious taste is the taste of a ritualized meal community or the taste of certain dishes or food items that have a ritual or symbolic effect. Mulled wine, turkey, gingerbread and big meals are all elements of the ritual structure around 'Christmas', defining not only the season but also those who celebrate it.

This means that we can distinguish between two different ways of talking about religious taste. One takes its point of departure in food and meals with a focus on the transcendent effect of the meal or the individual dish, while the other focuses on the function of food or meals as a ritual community, which—with reference to a holy principle—creates religious identity. In the former way of talking about religious taste, the code is 'immanence/transcendence', because the immanence of the food or meal is the basis of a transcendent experience. In the latter, the code is 'us/them' because the food, the specific food item or the meal as a whole is the basis of religious identity, i.e. an identity tied to something that is positioned beyond the community and therefore cannot be discussed.

With a point of departure in the transcendent effect, the code 'immanence/ transcendence' can be used to communicate about food and meals. A certain taste or meal is heavenly or divine if it contains qualities that cause it to transcend itself. The food is not just 'delicious' or 'healthy'; it transcends common experience and thereby becomes trans-empiric. We may experience a heavenly or spiritual community. In a Christian context, the best known example is probably communion, which is repeated during church services when the celebrant at the altar refers to the bread as 'the body of Christ' and the wine as 'the blood of Christ'. This ascribes a symbolic function to the meal, according to some modern Lutherans, because it symbolizes something other than itself. However, according to the Catholic Church, a literal transformation takes place: the bread and wine are transformed into the body and blood of Christ. Whatever the view, the relation between immanence and transcendence, i.e. between worldly and otherworldly, is interpreted literally in that the otherworldly is represented or incarnated in bread and wine.

Taking the ritualizing function of food as a starting point, religious taste can occur if the food and meal are part of religious rituals. Here, the code 'us/them' is relevant in terms of religious identity. When, for example, we eat together and abide by specific ritual rules, we may refer to an otherworldly phenomenon; however, what we really do is celebrate ourselves i.e. the community, and thereby strengthen social coherence. Religious festivals are evidence of this: Christmas dinner marks the beginning of a Christmas ritual, and Easter lunch, although originally marking the resurrection of Christ, is a meal that mainly serves to create a sense of community. For some, it refers to something holy and indisputable; for others, it is merely a recurrent tradition.

Meals and meal culture can also be religiously motivated in other ways: during Lent, for instance, Christians commemorate the forty days Jesus spent in the desert; in the Catholic and Orthodox traditions in particular, it is an important time in which people abstain from eating meat and prepare for Easter. Fasting followed by a celebrative meal in accordance with religious precepts is a phenomenon known from almost all religions, where the effect of absence of food echoes the subsequent meal. Fasting creates a distance to mundane taste experiences at the same time as heightening expectations of the first meal following the end of fasting. Today, in a cultural Christian context, fasting and the end of the fasting period is first and foremost a ritual that creates social coherence, and only few people eat different fasting foods and are aware of the original intention of preparing people for the following days of fasting.

Jewish Taste and Meals as an Example

For modern Jews, religious taste is a practical matter. In other words, it is more connected to the understanding of religion as expressed by Durkheim than Luhmann. In Judaism, taste is not about something divine or transcendent but about the mundane. Judaism is rooted in the mundane. Taste plays a central role, and meals are important rituals of a non-holy nature. Community is the main point of meals, and festivals are especially important. As much as possible, all food is made from scratch and everyone comes together to eat it. Some dishes are symbolic, and there are different ways of preparing them that represent familial, historical, regional and cultural traditions.

There are many ritual precepts related to the meals, and taste is rooted—and establishes roots—in history and identity. As Durkheim said, it ensures societal coherence. Ingredient combinations are important; for example, meat and dairy must be kept separate. The same goes for shellfish and pork. Such rules may seem rigid, and for progressive Jews it is fully religiously acceptable to compromise if required by lifestyle, place or living conditions. For orthodox and conservative Jews, however, it is important to abide by 'kosher', i.e. the traditionally and ritually based rules for food and meals. Progressive Jews have a higher degree of 'freedom' to live in accordance with the culture they are part of without feeling that they betray the religious food and meal precepts. It is central to them to enjoy food in a community and thus bring about shared associations.

Jewish food and meals are good examples of what we call religious taste because, due to their ritual structure and symbolism, they are ascribed religious significance that creates a framework around the identity, culture and memory of the congregation. Different branches of Judaism have their own culture in which meals must be prepared and taste like meals the followers grew up with. These branches focus on which meals and dishes to hold on to in order to continue tradition and/or faith. For instance, they experience that eating brings them closer to life, love and their fellow human beings. This is expressed through a specific kind of bread, candle and prayer, just like the taste of the wine and the salt on the bread are significant in regard to the religious experience and community. In some cases, the symbols become highly literal: signs of something other in the sense that they resemble what they symbolize. For progressive Jews, religion is primarily a question of compassion and ethics. God is, so to speak, expressed through human relations and practices. Many progressive Jews may not be 'religious' in a literal sense, but they still see themselves as Jews on the basis of cultural values, history, ethics, etc.

Different festivals are central to Jewish taste: Rosh Hashanah (head/ beginning of the year) marks the beginning of the year in the Jewish calendar. Rosh Hashanah is celebrated with honey cake and apples dipped in honey, which symbolizes the wish for the year to be good, mellow and sweet. Challah bread, which is eaten on shabbat, i.e. the Jewish day of rest that begins at sunset on Friday and ends at sunset on Saturday, is made in a round shape at Rosh Hashanah. The round bread symbolizes the passing of the year. The one or two days around Rosh Hashanah are holidays for all Jews, who use them to go to the synagogue or spend time with their family. Food is a central element of all Jewish holidays, and Rosh Hashanah is no exception. The food has a symbolic meaning at the same time as referring directly to the stories in which the holiday is mentioned. The sweet, round taste is key to the New Year's celebration, whereas unfermented bread is important in relation to Pesach.

Pesach in spring is another religious festival. It lasts eight days and begins with reading about the story of the Jewish being enslaved in Egypt. The stories about the emancipation from Egypt are related to taste. The food eaten during the festival reflects the stories about enslavement and cruelty. Therefore, it is a tradition to eat horse radish because it provokes tears, and in that sense the taste experience literally conveys a sense of how hard it was to be a slave. During these seven days, only unleavened bread can be eaten, in commemoration of the days when there was no time to finish the bread. Religious taste is about recalling stories and identity. They must 're-enter' the body, reminding people about what it was like to be a slave in Egypt.

The end of Shabbat is marked with a ritual in which a group of people smell a box of spices that is passed around. The smell of the spices points towards the future, anticipating a week without fasting. After the fasting period of Yom Kippur, the intensity of flavors is heightened: "It is fantastic to eat after having fasted for 27 hours".

Religious taste is linked in several ways to the food associated with the Jewish holidays. Fasting represents a sacrifice of the mundane, and the idea of taste causes longing for that which awaits and can be met with renewed power and hope. Pesach calls for suffering through taste, and thus for solidarity with historical suffering. Festive meals refer to the religious. We have survived: let us eat. And perhaps also: we survive by eating. Food should be plentiful. A Jewish mother is a loving mother who cooks plenty of food. Here, religious taste is linked to loving taste, which will be elaborated on below.

Even though some main ingredients are recurrent, is the food eaten in connection with the holidays varies. Food and eating in Judaism are strongly connected to a person's position in the world. Food is a carrier of identity, just as it is determined by family and place. Nevertheless, many Jews who are not 'orthodox' adopt certain foods, such as bagels, that subsequently become an integrated part of the food culture of the surrounding society.

Taste, Cosmology and Other Religious Rituals as Examples

The following is based on first-hand communication with Yoshihiro Murata, head chef at one of Japan's most famous restaurants, Kikunoi Restaurant in Kyoto (in fact, there are three restaurants: Ryotei Kikunoi (Kyoto, three Michelin stars), Akasaka Kikunoi (Tokyo, two Michelin stars) and Roan Kikunoi (Kyoto, two Michelin stars)). According to Murata, food, cooking and gastronomy in Japan are based on religious cosmology to a larger degree than in Europe. It might make sense to distinguish between a secular European kitchen and a religious Japanese kitchen. The foundation for the Japanese kitchen is the idea of extraction, i.e. that all ingredients or 'substances' are rooted in the divine and should be prepared so as to subtract the divine. What is extracted is the taste of the ingredient. Taste is therefore holy or an expression of the holy.

But also, the substance used to subtract is holy. For instance, the perception is that water comes from the holy and that it is therefore a holy subtraction to clean, rinse and boil food in water. For the same reason, boiling is preferred to frying in butter or oil. Rice is a basic and holy ingredient because it grows in water, contains 60 % water and is boiled in water. Water, 'translated' into the system of taste presented in this book, represents taste 'as such', i.e. the taste that has no flavor but adds flavor to other ingredients. In the Japanese kitchen, water is both a holy means of subtraction and an expression of the holy taste.

Based on this mentality, it is possible to imagine a wealth of dimensions of taste related to religious cosmology: the water encapsulates the divine, whereas the different dimensions of taste represent the divine in its many emanations. They emanate from God, so to speak. Therefore, a meal should contain a multitude of taste emanations that are different but at the same time point back to the religious communality. The Japanese bentõ-bako (lunch box), which in its ideal version contains 46 elements of food, is a good example of this mentality (the same goes for traditional meals with their variety of small dishes and taste experiences); in the divine bentõ-bako, the holy is manifested in its basic form, both in the rice and many other manifestations. The central taste is umami, which is, for instance, created by using dashi as a basic ingredient. Dashi is produced from katsuobushi, which is finely shredded pieces of dried, fermented fish that are boiled in water and used as what, in a European context, would be called stock. Dashi is used for boiling noodles and as a basis for meat and vegetable soups, as well as many other dishes. As Yoshihiro Murata says, "Dashi is pure umami water."

Meals also unfold as religious rituals. Upmarket restaurants present themselves as sanctuaries. Shoes must be left at the entrance; food is prepared and served by the chefs, and the whole course of events is highly ritualized. Whether something tastes good or bad is not determined by secularized taste judgements but by judgement of how closely the taste and taste combinations approach the divine. Very generalized, it can be said that the Kantian system of judgement has a fully realized alternative in the shape of the religious Japanese taste system.

A good example of ritualistic meals can be found in the Japanese tea ceremony, which is a unique tradition developed to create a space for spiritual cleansing. The ceremony has roots in the 12th century, when Zen Buddhists recorded the procedure of a cleansing tea ceremony. Therefore, the ceremony takes place according to carefully planned and essential rules designed to help the participants forget the stress of everyday life and focus on spiritual cleansing.

Of course, there are many other religiously based taste cosmologies around the world. The Indian kitchen, with its many basic tastes referring to a system of gods, is an apt example (Howes, 2010). Religious meal rituals are also numerous. One example is the use of basil in religious ceremonies in Greece, where a sprig of basil is dipped in holy water and shaken over the head of the person receiving the blessing. Therefore, basil is usually not used in daily cooking; it tastes too much of the holy or is viewed as too holy to be used on an everyday basis (Sutton & Vournelis, 2009). This is a contrast to the Japanese kitchen, where water as mentioned is used as much as possible because it represents the utmost divine. Another example is foods used in death rituals, like food that is carried around on Halloween to commemorate the dead. Afterwards, the food is left for the dead to enjoy. According to tradition, the dead absorb the taste, which is why the food loses its flavor and smell (Sutton & Vournelis, 2009).

Teaching Example: Religious Taste

Religious taste is a fruitful teaching theme that relates to the composition of both food and meals. The students can work with religious food and meal cultures, focusing on the composition of meals for religious holidays and festivals, and on the guiding principles. Regarding reflections on religious taste, focus can be placed on contemporary and historical as well as geographical differences between religious persuasions, and how religious food and meal cultures develop and influence each other in various 'holy' contexts. The students can work with the composition of meals based on different criteria, for example everyday life, tradition, celebration, etc. With a starting point in religious everyday meals and/ or special religious meals, they can investigate the composition of a meal according to occasion, host, symbols, participants, space, time and the food itself. By presenting and serving different dishes and meals, they focus on the impact of presentation, mood, participants, time, place and occasion on religious taste. The religious history of the meal is a study area in itself. The students can work with defining taste in a religious-historical and theological perspective.

By drawing on their own meal experiences, the students can compare food and meal cultures from different religions, eras and places. Knowledge of the development of religious taste from, for example, the Medieval period to the Renaissance, or from the bourgeois kitchen to national romanticism in the nineteenth century, can create a basis for the students' understanding of the religious taste they are part of. They can work with historical and global religious food cultures and their influence on contemporary local food cultures, or with understanding religious meals from different kitchens with long-standing food traditions, and intricately developed meal traditions, e.g. the Jewish, Muslim, Christian and Hindu kitchens.

Time, socialization and taste experiences are integral parts of religious food culture. With a point of departure in everyday religious meals and, subsequently, in special meals, the students can study the composition of a meal according to occasion, history, symbols, sensory experiences, participants, space, time and food itself. Through preparing and serving different dishes and meals, they focus on the impact of presentation, mood and when, where and how the food is served and received.

Focus on differences between religious cultures, past and present, and in different parts of the world, and how food and meals develop and influence each other, means that teaching should include food and meals in religious, social, multicultural and historical perspectives. Religiosity is not an unambiguous concept. Religious taste represents a system of rules and conventions for when, what, how and with whom we eat. There is an obvious structural link between moral and religious taste. Within a specific faith, the norms define what is 'right' and 'wrong' in terms of eating. The religious norms are different, e.g. between nations, social groups, age groups and genders, and contribute to emphasizing communities of taste within a religion and to demarcating cultures. Religious taste is, therefore, closely linked to human identity, not least because 'the holy' is indisputable.

Something unique to religious taste is the fasting period, which is not, contrary to one might think, necessarily a period of non-tasting. During the 30 days of the Muslim Ramadan, the morning meal Suhoor is served every day before sunbreak and after sunset, the Iftar, or the breaking of the fast, is shared. In many cultures across the world, the breaking of the fast is a source of great gastronomic pleasure and diversity. Typically, the Iftar meal is introduced with dates and then followed by a number of traditional meals shared together with family, friends and other fellow believers in the local mosque. Here, the taste is essentially religious, transcending the normal meals, also because the senses are sharpened after a day of fasting. The Muslim Ramadan is concluded with *id al-fitr*, which is a euphoria of flavor: extended families get together, each contributing a dish, to take part in the meal. Something similar happens after the 40 days of fasting in the Christian tradition, which are followed by the Easter feast. The students can work with taste in connection with the end of 'purification', and students with a Christian background can, for example, interview students with a Muslim background who abide by these rules in order to better understand the transcendentality of religious taste and the euphoric sense of flavor succeeding a fasting period.

LOVING TASTE

Dimension of taste	Code	Symbolically generalized medium	Reflection repertoire
Loving taste	+/- Love	Love/ passion	Knowledge about love articulated through food/meals

> This woman is now turning a dinner into a kind of love affair, into a love affair of the noble and romantic category in which one no longer distinguishes between bodily and spiritual appetite or satiety (Blixen, 1958:65).

This is how the retired General Löwenhielm recalls Colonel Galliffet talking about the female head chef at Café Anglais in Paris in Karen Blixen's *Babette's Feast*. After the defeat of the Paris Commune in 1871, she flees to Berlevaag, where she displays her cooking skills one last time to the benefit of twelve guests in the small provincial town in northern Norway. She turns the meal into a love affair.

Babette's Feast is a literary condensation of loving taste, i.e. a meal and dishes that taste of love. The love relation can go two ways. First, it can be a relation between the one who cooks the meal and the one or more people who eat it. The chef or the person cooking uses the food and the meal as a medium to express their love. The food and meal constitute a declaration of love expressed through taste. Second, the food and meal make up a framework for a love relation between those who eat. The meal can be a framework for parental love or romantic seduction. In both cases, the code is 'love/ no love'. The food, meal and presentation let the receiver sense (taste, see, smell, hear and feel) whether the cook has expressed their love.

In connection with children's meals and cookbooks, it is often the parents who express their love through food. One particularly characteristic example is the packed lunch, because the child producing it from their schoolbag is in reality producing a love letter. In the book *The Little Green Book for Packed Lunch Eaters*, the author writes that a packed lunch not only has to heighten our spirits; it has to contain "fresh ingredients and love", which is why it should be "prepared with care" (Skaarup, 2012).

As we wrote in Part One on the history of children's cookbooks, the dimension of love was introduced in the Danish associate professor Helle Brønnum Carlsen's *Yum, Love to the Last Bite*, published in 1998, a cookbook for adults featuring food for children. The message was that children's sense of taste should be taken seriously and discussed and developed together with them. Meals are not only about nutrition and cleanliness but just as much about love and responsiveness. It is characteristic of many children's cookbooks published since 2000, that the emphasis is on tastiness, passion and pleasure, and always with the meal as a medium to communicate love, either implicitly or explicitly, from cooking to meal communities. For example, *Rosita & Franciska's Bistro*, states that "the worst thing Rosita knows is food that doesn't contain love" (Olsen et al., 2016: 153). Another example is a cookbook from 2014, *The Favorite Dishes of Much-wanted Children*, which has the subtitle *Kiss Fussiness Goodbye*. The authors establish that healthy meals are prepared out of love for the children and that if parents' greatest wish is for their "children to become happy", they need to "create the framework for a healthy lifestyle" (Thorhauge & Hundebøll, 2014: 10). Everything is about "love, home and hearth" (Thorhauge & Hundebøll, 2014: 3). The cost, in relation to the ideal of creative children conquering the kitchen, is that the mothers and perhaps fathers (who, however, are absent in the book) must reconquer the kitchen. How is it possible to express love of one's children through food if they cook it themselves?

Loving taste is a result of both individual dishes and meal communities. In terms of taste, the taste elements need to be balanced so that the dish is not too bitter, sour or salty, and the mouthfeel should be soft and seductive. The community should be intimate and arranged to avoid distracting elements. In children's popular culture, the meal in Walt Disney's *Lady and the Tramp* is an archetypical example: Spaghetti Bolognese served under a starlit sky, and with an accordion-playing chef in the background, creates a framework for seduction, and the food is bursting with love for the eating guests.

A very concrete example of food and meals as frameworks for seduction is *The Pulling Cookbook* from 2016. As mentioned in the introduction, it contains "50 delicious recipes and lots of tips, all developed with the aim of you hitting a homerun on the first date" (Hansen, 2016).

The tone is very different in Karen Blixen's prose; her loving taste community is clearly not aimed at 'homeruns' or 'dating', but rather at creating a passionate community that is structurally linked to the religious. As Babette's wines and dishes are presented, the taciturn Norwegian feast transforms into a transcendent community:

> None of the 17 guests later on had any clear remembrance of it. They only knew that the rooms had been filled with a heavenly light, as if a number of small halos had blended into one glorious radiance. Taciturn old people received the gift of tongues; ears that for years had been almost deaf were opened to it. Time itself had merged into eternity. Long after midnight the windows of the house shone like gold, and golden song flowed out into the winter air (Blixen, 1958:67).

However, examples of loving taste are not only found in prose but also in everyday contexts. Love of children, friends and family is also expressed through daily cooking or crammed into the children's packed lunches. One example of the influence of loving taste is found in the many food and meal policies developed by day care centers and many schools. Parents are usually strongly involved in developing these policies: what should be served and how; should there be guidelines regarding the children's packed lunches, and can the children taste each other's food? The parents' involvement is in itself a declaration of love that should not 'get lost' in the institutionally formalized procedures. Discussions often come to a head when introducing school lunch programs. In principle, it would be health promoting and have an effect on equality if all children ate the food served by the school. The cost, however, would be the loss of the packed lunch as the parents' personal message to their children.

The same issue is encountered with regard to whether children in kindergartens are allowed to taste each other's packed lunches. Obviously, it is a good idea if the aim is to stimulate the children's curiosity about food; however, the problem is that it gets in the way of the packed lunch as a declaration of love. Love cannot be shared: this is 'my' packed lunch for 'my' child, not for the entire group of children. For the same reason, parents are often particularly careful when preparing food for their children's birthday parties: it presents an opportunity for the parents to show the whole institution or class how much they love their child.

There are also interesting and complex examples of structural links between the love and health codes, cf. the above-mentioned book by Thorhauge and Hundebøll (2014). However, the relationship between the two cannot be expressed quite as simply as the authors wish. On the one hand, parents' love is expressed through their desire for their child to eat healthily; carrots in the packed lunch, rather than chocolate, are a structurally linked expression of love: I love you; therefore, your food should be healthy. On the other hand, the two codes can also get in each other's way: consideration of the child's health may get in the way of loving expression if the loving taste is defined by sweet taste and a soft mouthfeel. Sweetness and softness are nowhere to be found if the packed lunch consist of carrots, cucumber and chicken nuggets or sticks.

Teaching Example: Loving Taste

Teaching loving taste can focus on the students' own loving taste experiences, including judgement criteria for the code 'love/ no love'. Loving taste is not expressed conceptually, but the students need to develop a professional language to cover loving communication in order to judge it. In a teaching context, this means that the students taste, smell, see, feel and put words to taste. They reflect on how their impressions are connected to emotions, personal experience and cultural norms and values, and what love means for their eating habits and meals. The ability to express themselves about loving taste can be developed by use of imagination and creativity; as the students acquire a repertoire of concepts for loving expressions and experience, they can experiment with developing recipes for dishes with loving taste and ways of serving love.

Teaching can focus on different factors that impact the loving taste experience, e.g. symbols in food linked to sensed taste by different sensory characteristics, and to where, when, how and with whom we eat. It will always be of crucial importance who cooks the food, and the students can work with different loving 'senders' and 'receivers.' They can also work with descriptions and interpretations of loving food and meals, and present them in class. Through this, the students work with both senders and receivers, i.e. loving taste in cooking, serving and eating.

Time, company and taste experiences are integral elements of loving taste. Based on everyday and special meals, loving taste can be investigated in relation to occasion, hosting, symbols, sensations, participants, space, time and food itself. Students can present and serve different dishes and meals and thereby focus on the significance, in terms of loving taste, of presentation, mood, time, surroundings and the way in which the food is eaten.

Loving taste is linked to meal culture, which can be defined as a system of rules and conventions for when, what, how and with whom we eat. Within a certain culture, the norms dictate what is right and wrong in connection to eating. Cultural norms are different, e.g. depending on nation, social group, age group and gender, and they contribute to denoting loving taste within the culture in question and to demarcating cultures. Culture is closely related to human identity.

Therefore, it is also important that the students reflect on how they represent different cultures of love. By drawing on their own meal experiences, they can compare loving taste from different exemplary areas. It is relevant to ask the following questions:

- Which times are we dealing with (historical time, time of day, week, year, life)?

- Which places are we dealing with, and how is loving taste influenced by values, including norms and material frameworks for food and meals?

- Which social environment (gender, class, age) is loving taste associated with?

TRENDY TASTE

Dimension of taste	Code	Symbolically generalized medium	Reflection repertoire
Trendy taste	+/- Trendy	Style	Knowledge about fashion and style expressed through food/meals

Participating in different food festivals can illustrate the meaning of trendy taste. If you had been in Copenhagen during summer 2017, you would have seen a plethora of stalls at the Street Food Festival. One stall was called All about Ostrich. It served "juicy ostrich burgers and crispy sweet potato fries". Another stall called Anatolia offered "authentic Turkish cuisine cooked with love". Banzai Street Sushi served "fresh sushi and oysters directly from our red food truck", and a stall from Berlin served "different kinds of burger, e.g. Surf 'n' Turf, Devil's Lax and much more" (Copenhagen Street Food, 2017). The different stalls had only two things in common: they were located on the Food Festival island, and they were counted among the trendiest places to go in Copenhagen that summer. Flavors and dishes were extremely diverse, yet they were united through trendy taste or by appealing to trendy taste.

Food and meals becoming trendy is not a phenomenon unique to food festivals. During the development of today's gastronomy, food has become trendy; within the area of gastronomy, restaurants and food critique, a social system has developed that echoes fashion in general as seen, for instance, in the clothing industry. It is important to be able to distinguish between what is trendy today and what was trendy yesterday. The paleo diet was trendy some years ago but is 'old school' today. Sushi was trendy at the beginning of the 00s but is slowly descending into the standard repertoire alongside pizza and tapas. The French, Italian and Spanish kitchens were replaced by the green kitchen, which, in turn, was replaced by New Nordic, leaving them as something we can return to like other fashion phenomena, ironically referring to them as 'retro' (Wistoft & Qvortrup, 2018b). This is one of the particular characteristics of fashion phenomena: we make our distinctions through the lens of time.

This entails that the symbolically generalized medium is style because, as Danish philosopher Lars-Henrik Schmidt has stated, "[t]he inert element of fashion is called style" (Schmidt, 1991: 47). What has style and what does not? How do we distinguish one style from another, and how do we relate a particular style to a particular time or era? That is the precondition for being able to communicate about fashion. Something is trendy because it is a style associated with the present. Something is not trendy if it is seen as representative of yesterday's style or that of last year or decade. The reflection repertoire is fashion and style because it entails what is trendy, and why we must know about styles, eras and what is 'in style'. Why is it trendy just now to eat pulled duck burgers and drink mojitos on deck chairs outside, and why will some people go somewhere else within a few months because the trend has waned or outlived itself, i.e. become mere style (and is therefore not trendy anymore)?

In fashion as a social system, there are also actors who become 'fashionable' because they represent today's trend. A group of so-called celebrity chefs, whose social capital is in high demand, has developed (cf. Bourdieu, see p. 98-99). There are several examples of this among the Danish children's cookbooks: already in 2003, Malene Grøndahl and Thomas Vinge published *Celebrity Goodies: Seven of the Coolest People Give you Their Best Recipes* (Grøndahl & Vinge, 2003), and in 2015, Maj-Britt Soll and Michael Saly asked five master chefs how they cook with and for their children, which resulted in a collection of recipes under the title *Food Within Children's Reach* (Soll & Saly, 2015). In 2016, the two young cookbook authors Rosita Evarista Buchardt Olsen and Franciska Dina Buchardt Olsen published *Rosita and Franciska's Bistro: Kitchen Skills for Teens and Other Young*

People who Love Parties and Food. Here, it is not only the food and meals that are trendy; the authors position themselves as trendy food masters:

> Franciska or "Franne", as most people call her, is a true master when it comes to baking. In just a minute, she can magically produce the most delicious cookies you have been craving all day. Franciska is a party animal; she loves dinners and parties and doesn't like to miss a single one. You always catch her lost in concentration when she is cooking, and often with a naughty pout. That's how she is. She cooks with style and she likes everything to be sumptuous, including herself (Olsen et al., 2016: 152).

The food writer Rosita is also stylish. She is characterized as "artistic, perfectionistic and systematic in a kitchen. She is the type of person who can take the simplest of dishes and make it special" (Olsen et al., 2016). Bistro food is trendy because it is a style associated with the present. And style is very much related to personality and self-promotion. Trendy taste is not only an indication of the style of the food but also the chefs.

Teaching Example: Trendy Taste

Trendy taste is an obvious subject in relation to media education, where the content is linked to food and meals across time. The students can be involved in the planning of the teaching, assuming that they are the ones who are most up to date when it comes to style and fashion. Therefore, the teacher should initiate a dialogue with the students to establish their starting point and expectations, and use these as a guideline to create a course design that points towards the teaching objectives for teaching 'trendy taste'. This entails that the students should have a large degree of influence on the teaching. Topics and content should be selected and arranged in collaboration between teacher and students to ensure that the students' style-related areas of interest are incorporated; at the same time, there has to be natural progression and coherence.

Trendy taste can be structurally linked to the six above-mentioned dimensions of taste to strengthen integration across teaching areas. As mentioned, teaching can benefit from being founded on the competences the students have acquired in IT and media education. The students can work with searching for trends and trendy taste in different eras, and developing models illustrating which food styles have dominated when. In relation to IT and media, the students can benefit from working with four student positions: a) as critical investigators; b) as analyzing receivers; c) as determined and creative producers; and d) as responsible participants. Emphasis can be placed on media representation techniques of cool and trendy food. The students can also focus on self-promotion, creativity and world views.

Out-of-school activities can also be included, for example trips to visit trendy food bloggers, so-called foodies, street food venues, etc., where the students can form substantiated opinions on what is trendy or not, and why.

The students can choose to include trendy taste as an approach to solving a general issue. For example, they can look into the influence of a particular everyday food as something that represents an upcoming and, at some point, waning tendency in gastro-national phenomena. Or they can work with so-called 'dogmatic food' on the basis of a critical assessment of what constitutes positive and negative dogma at a certain time. Why was the paleo diet allowed to contain some ingredients and not others? Were these ingredients in fact historically correct or did they rather represent and promote a fashion trend? What does it mean that ingredients must be 'local', and why is it that global food is promoted at trendy street food markets at the same time as the restaurant next door celebrates local produce and local food tradition?

Teaching Taste

PART THREE

Didactics of Taste

TASTE AS SUCH

Does taste as such exist? Immanuel Kant (1724-1804) would probably answer affirmatively: the world exists 'as such' or 'in itself', as a precondition for, and prior to, someone observing it (Kant, 2002 [1793]). In other words, Kant made the ontological claim that 'the world exists,' even though in principle it cannot be proved. In doing so, he opposed the constructivists of his time, for example the English philosopher George Berkeley (1685-1753), who argued that we know nothing except what we can see, which, according to Berkeley, is another way of saying that nothings exist that we cannot see. The Austrian-English philosopher Ludwig Wittgenstein (1889-1951) attempted to reach a compromise at the beginning of the 20th century: "whereof one cannot speak, thereof one must be silent" (Wittgenstein, 1969 [1921]). In other words, there are two positions and a compromise: Kant claims that 'the thing as such' exists; Berkeley claims that nothing exists that we cannot see; Wittgenstein says that we must remain silent about that of which we cannot speak.

Niklas Luhmann has a different approach to this fundamental philosophical problem. He says that it should not be handled ontologically but epistemologically. We do not know anything about the world in itself, but we do know that any observation entails a blind spot: the observer cannot observe their own observation (Luhmann, 1990; cf. also Thyssen, 2003). Similarly, we can say about taste: the person who tastes cannot taste their own taste; they cannot put themselves in a position outside their own taste. Whereas Kant argues ontologically (about the 'being' of the world), Luhmann argues epistemologically (about the way in which we make observations). However, in our view, the same conclusion can be drawn: it makes sense to claim that taste 'as such' exists as a thing or quality in itself (Kant), or as a pure taste experience that precedes all manners of perceiving taste (Luhmann), for example because it is not a bodily and conceptualized experience.

Forms of Taste

In other words, there is good reason to assume that taste exists in itself; however, we cannot say anything about taste as such taste before tasting, so to speak. Taste only becomes interesting when we approach the question of how taste is observed, because it is dependent on 'observation of taste' (a term we use instead of Kant's 'view of taste'). We have already seen lots of examples above: the sensory scientist tastes in one way, the health professional in another and the ethicist in a third. What the sensory scientist tastes as 'salty' or 'sour', the health professional tastes as 'healthy' or 'unhealthy', while the ethicist tastes it as good or bad animal welfare. These modes of observation are in other words self-referential or 'autopoietic': the sensory scientists refer to their own sensory modes of taste, while the ethicists refer to their moral taste criteria.

However, as we have also seen, the different modes of observation can also be combined and lend structure to each other through what we call 'structural links', borrowing a term from systems theory. The aestheticians, for example, uses the terms 'sour', 'sweet', 'salty', 'bitter' and 'umami' from sensory science when making their judgement of taste, at the same time as these terms are merely the descriptive precondition for the aesthetic judgement: does this taste delicious or not, and why? A good example of institutional and systematic structural links between sensory science and taste aesthetics (i.e. gastronomy) is the subject of gastrophysics, which combines sensory science and gastronomy.

Nevertheless, these modes of taste observation referred to as dimensions of taste can be grouped together in small or large units. Three of these units can be termed Kantian, sociological and phenomenological modes of taste observation. Taste is perceived in one way through Kant's epistemological theory, whereas it is perceived differently through the lens of sociology or phenomenology.

A Kantian Theory of Taste

According to Kant, we can make different types of judgement in relation to an object. We can talk about the shape, weight, size and extent of the object. In that case, we are referring to what is termed 'objective' properties. But we can also talk about what is termed the 'subjective' properties: is the object beautiful, appealing, attractive, tasty, etc.? In that case, we are not talking about the object itself but about our desire in relation to the object. When we express desire, we use our sense of taste. "The ability to judge through such desire is taste" (Kant, 1971 [1790]: 50 f.). Kant calls the judgement of taste an aesthetic judgement (Kant, 1971 [1790]: 67 f.). According to Kant, the pleasure that is defined by the judgement of taste is disinterested, i.e. not politically motivated: we may perceive a film or a painting as beautiful or attractive, even if we do not agree on its political statement (Kant, 1971 [1790]: 69 f.), and even though we cannot derive pleasure from the 'good', i.e. the 'interest' or political statement, of the object in question (Kant, 1971 [1790]: 73-76).

When we make a judgement of taste, it is fundamentally subjective: I think this dish tastes good. But being able to make a subjective judgement in a manner that makes sense requires common, i.e. social, judgements of taste. When we make judgements of taste, we have to relate reflectively to the judgements of others (Kant, 1971 [1790]: 214). We make use of what Kant calls sensus communis: for example, when we gather around the table, taste a particular dish, smell it, feel it in our mouth, look at its structures and colors and share these sense impressions with each other. In fact, we cannot make judgements of taste without presupposing the idea of a community of taste, because it is not possible to speak purely subjectively to or with others, just as others cannot agree or disagree on our judgement without the existence of such a community (Kant, 1971 [1790]: 123 f.). However, the precondition is subjective investment, a statement of 'this is how I see things'. In Kant's slightly convoluted phrasing: "The necessity of the universal assent that is thought in a judgement of taste, is a subjective necessity which, under the presupposition of a common sense, is represented as objective" (Kant, 1952 [1790]: 84).

Translating all this into taste in food, we can conclude that, according to Kant, we judge the taste of a dish or meal aesthetically. Whether a specific dish, e.g. foie gras, is tasty or not, i.e. produces pleasant or unpleasant flavor, is a judgement that can be made regardless of the implicit political message or core value of the dish. We can also enjoy that the dish tastes of animal welfare or fair trade. In that case, we enjoy that the political core value is in keeping with our own.

When we taste something and judge our taste experience, we do it subjectively but on the condition of the existence of a community of taste. The statement 'I think this tastes wonderful' only makes sense when others can discuss the premises for the statement and dispute the judgement. However, this does not mean that taste is objective: it means that we must all invest our taste experiences in the common discussion of taste in order to make socially valid judgements.

The reason why we support Kant's philosophy of taste in this book is that we share the idea and ideal of a person making and substantiating a judgement of taste as a competent individual. Nevertheless, Kant's philosophy of taste is also problematic in the present context in that it limits taste to aesthetic taste, even if there are certain links to moral taste and to arguments drawn from other dimensions of taste. In other words, we think that Kant's concept of taste is too narrow. Others have stated that it is also too 'rational'. It is not without reason that Kant's philosophy is rooted in the European era of enlightenment. The question is whether taste and judgements of taste are always as rational as they are made out to be when translated and substantiated. This question has been raised in one way by the French sociologist Pierre Bourdieu (1930-2002) and in another by the Danish philosopher Lars-Henrik Schmidt. Pierre Bourdieu disputes the ideal of making generally valid judgements. Instead, he points to sociology as an area that enhances the understanding of judgements of taste as indications of the social position of the person making them. Lars-Henrik Schmidt writes that there is too little sensuousness in Kant. In order to establish an understanding of the impact of sensuousness in relation to judgements of taste, we can benefit from turning to phenomenological philosophy (Schmidt, 1991). Bourdieu's and Schmidt's positions will be briefly presented in the two following sections.

Sociological Theory of Taste[2]

Many cultural researchers and sociologists have offered their opinion on what taste is and how taste and judgements of taste function socially. They often focus on the

---

[2] This section is based on Leer & Wistoft 2015, p. 20-21.

significance and function ascribed to taste in different contexts, and on how taste forms part of social and cultural systems of communication.

One of the most thorough and debated contributions to modern sociological research on food is without doubt that presented by Pierre Bourdieu in his book *La distinction* (1979). Bourdieu's point is that taste does not reflect the individual's unique physiological taste, and that individual judgements of taste cannot be summarized in a common, generally valid judgement. On the contrary, Bourdieu claims that the individual's judgement of taste reflects their social position and background: "Taste classifies the one who classifies", writes Bourdieu with a maxim that condenses his analysis (Bourdieu, 1979: VI). Hence, taste is an art of differentiation, where taste and not least distaste function distinctively within the classes in a social process through which the different classes become distinct from each other. The cultivation of specific taste ideals creates a collective identity within the group. A good example is Christmas dinner: some swear by the traditional Danish pork roast, perhaps accompanied by traditional pork sausage; others eat duck; a third group prefers turkey, while a fourth group celebrates a vegan Christmas. For all groups, the choice of food is a marker of social identity. This kind of food community often has a negative function: what we prefer seems natural, while what others prefer comes across as almost abhorrent. Bourdieu stresses that "social identity is defined and confirmed in the difference" (Bourdieu, 1979: 191); taste is one of the strongest and most important markers of difference, partly because our own taste preferences are so hard to put to one side or disregard. In some instances, it makes sense to talk about 'taste regimes', i.e. groups of people who gather around and draw identity from specific taste ideals.

The distinct function of the many 'taste regimes' is to judge, understand and communicate in everyday social interaction: when we look into the shopping baskets of those in front of us at the checkout; when we choose between organic and non-organic food items; when we choose what food to bring for lunch at work, etc. However, it should be mentioned that there has been a change since the 1970s when Bourdieu wrote his book. The frameworks and boundaries between the social strata have become more fluid when it comes to ideals of taste, in pace with the growing middle class and increased access to a great variety of foods.

This can be seen as a form of democratized food culture, as the Canadian sociologists Josée Johnston and Shyon Bauman point out in *Foodies: Democracy and Distinction in The Gourmet Foodscape* (Johnston & Bauman, 2014). However, the authors also stress that this is by no means an indication that everything is of equal value. New taste hierarchies and taste codes are quickly emerging, not least in the booming 'foodie culture', where a cultural (and financial) upper class is using food culture to achieve status. The same tendency can be observed in the celebrated Nordic Cuisine, the popularity of 'street food', etc. Only trendy people 'get' trendy food. So even though the codes and understandings of 'good' and 'bad' – pleasant and unpleasant – taste have become less pronounced and more open to negotiation than in the strictly class-structured society described by Bourdieu, the idea that taste separates social groups is still valid.

The Bourdieu-inspired tradition of food and taste studies briefly presented here analyzes how taste functions as a means of communication and negotiation in social contexts. This branch of study often looks critically at how taste expressions and codes function as classifiers, and how food cultures and their different taste ideals denote social inequality in that they underline and cement hierarchies and boundaries between social groups. With a term taken from Bourdieu, we can say that food cultures become 'food regimes.'

One of the points that can be criticized in Bourdieu's theory of taste is that it leaves no room for the individual experience and the bodily occurrence that also constitutes the tasting process. There is no room for the sensuous, other than as a result of social identity. Even though this is a valid objection, we find that it is important to hold on to the point that the senses taste experience is always part of a social connection from which it cannot be separated. Nature and culture, experience and upbringing, will always be inextricably entangled in the taste experience.

Nevertheless, judgements of taste are not only the outcome of social identity; they are also the outcome of bodily experiences. This brings us to the second objection to Kant's philosophy of taste: there is too much sensibility and too little sensuousness in Kant. This point of view is advocated in phenomenological theory of taste.

Phenomenological Theory of Taste

In an article on "Philosophical Understandings of Taste", the Danish philosopher Liselotte Hedegaard promotes an understanding based on phenomenology (Hedegaard, 2017). The reason being that phenomenology strives to describe the bodily through the world as it unfolds in a first-person perspective, cf. one of the key works of phenomenology, Maurice Merleau-Ponty's *Phénomenologie de la perception* (Merleau-Ponty, 1945). What happens when an individual eats a dish? First, we use our sense of sight, then we use our sense of touch to judge the shape and consistency. After this, the sense of smell is activated, finally followed by step four: taking a bite, activating the sense of hearing, e.g. when chewing brings out a crunching sound, mouthfeel, and sense of consistency and taste when the food comes into contact with the taste receptors in out mouth.

Is this different from what the sensory scientist would say? Yes, according to Liselotte Hedegaard, because in this perspective, taste is not described in rational terms like both a sensory scientist and a rationally theoretic Kantian would express it to make an objective or subjective judgement. Phenomenological theory works its way to the pre-conceptual level, which, in the nature of things, evades rational explanation. Translated to Luhmann's systems theory, it means that the mental system, or perhaps the bodily-mental system, observes the world from a pre-linguistic perspective, and that these pre-linguistic observations only become socially valid when they, using language as a social linking tool, transform these experiences to fit the world of social communication.

In his book *Smagens analytik* (*Analytics of Taste*), Lars-Henrik Schmidt applies the same approach (Schmidt, 1991), taking his point of departure in Kant's philosophy, but 'quarantining' rationality, as he expresses it. Drawing inspiration from the German philosopher Friedrich Nietzsche (1844-1900), he claims that aesthetics and aesthetic judgement cannot be used as a parallel to rational judgement: "Aesthetics is physiology in use" (Schmidt, 1991: 17). In other words, aesthetics does not spring from rationality but from the bodily senses, which it systematizes and makes conceptual. Therefore, aesthetics is not based on rational arguments but on sensory impressions and dramaturgic arguments. However, in contrast to Liselotte Hedegaard, Schmidt does not believe that it prevents the taste analysis from producing general judgements of taste. On the contrary, his intention is to develop the outline of "a generalized and speculative physiology" (Schmidt, 1991: 17).

Succinctly put, his critique of Kant is that taste in Kant's aesthetics is a property of the power of judgement that makes us able to distinguish between desire and the opposite. But, he adds, "when Kant performs the fatal separation of sensuousness, splitting sense and imagination, he simultaneously precludes a sensuous phenomenologist philosophy, leaving himself at the mercy of an intellectualistic, meditative philosophy" (Schmidt, 1991: 30-31; our translation).

As mentioned, Lars-Henrik Schmidt's agenda is to develop a generalized and speculative physiology, i.e. a theory of the senses. It has to be generalized because he will not settle for the subjective judgement of taste; he wants to be able to generalize it to a common or, as he calls it, vulgar judgement of taste, e.g. as it unfolds during meals and social communication. It has to be speculative because his aim is speculative, rather than natural scientific, physiology.

On this basis, Schmidt develops a model of taste that is not empiric, like the seven dimensions of taste in the present book, but speculative. The model consists of a number of taste elements of which the first six are: feeling, taste, smell, touch, sight and hearing. In addition, there are three elements that all relate to the organization of the way in which the person tasting relates to themselves: proprioception (feeling of self), imagination and balance (harmony). Finally, there are some 'super-sensory' senses, i.e. the senses that belong to the "range of radiance" (Schmidt, 1991: 61): a sense for sex, a magnetic sense and a sense for love, which Schmidt calls narcissism. But, as he adds, "in order not to claim any scientific validity of this speculation, we must specify that these experiences come into effect, and their super-historical scheme may be constructed, even though physiological and psychological science cannot confirm the model" (Schmidt, 1991: 62).

We share the phenomenological interest in a broad concept of taste; however, as seen, we would like to make it even broader than the one suggested by Liselotte Hedegaard as inspired by Merleau-Ponty. This is why the sensory-phenomenological dimension of taste is only one of seven dimensions of taste. This expansion of the repertoire of taste resembles Lars-Henrik Schmidt's suggested dimensions of taste. However, we do not follow Schmidt's "speculative", as he terms it, expansion of the taste repertoire to twelve dimensions. Our expansion is empiric, and the number of dimensions is therefore rooted in an empirical approach rather than a metaphysical model of taste.

In addition, our main interest is invested in making taste experiences available through communication. In this respect, there are also similarities between our project and Schmidt's, although we use radically different terms. We do not stop at 'everybody to their own taste' or, in French, 'chacun à son goût'. Obviously, taste preferences are individual, i.e. in principle incommunicable; yet, we constantly share taste experiences. Therefore, we want to go beyond individual, subjective taste experiences, however vividly they may be explained through phenomenology. We are interested in the process through which taste is made communicatively available, i.e. part of and shared in social community, and through which it becomes the object of judgements of taste based on power of judgement.

From System of Taste to Didactics of Taste

The main philosophical inspiration for this book is Immanuel Kant and his focus on the competent citizen. However, 'our' version of Kant is not ontological. We do not presuppose that there is such a thing as 'the thing in itself'—in this case, 'taste in itself'—which is hidden from us until revealed through the different dimensions of taste. Our approach is epistemological, meaning that 'the thing in itself' must be re-described as the blind spot of observation: the unobservable precondition for observation. In the didactics of taste, it is taste as such, i.e. the observation of taste or taste experience, which is the blind spot. We anticipate criticism by stating that, in light of this, we should not talk about taste as a pure quality, or about dimensions of taste, because it sounds too ontological. Rather, we should talk about 'the blind spot of taste' and about 'modes of observation'. However, we have refrained from these terms for practical reasons, simply because they become overly 'obscure'.

Anyway, back to Kant. We found inspiration in his philosophy because we wanted to support the development of judgement of taste, or, to put it differently, to contribute to the development of taste competence. Just like it is important to be politically, morally and socially competent, it is important to be competent in a taste perspective, i.e. capable of making judgements of taste and substantiating and reflecting on them. Kant introduces his article "What is Enlightenment?" with the famous expression "Sapere aude!" In English: "Have the courage to use your own understanding!" (Kant, 1993 [1783]). And, we may add: the courage to be able to substantiate and reflect on it as a citizen in interaction with other citizens.

Kant focuses on the citizen as a political citizen. However, it is just as important to be a taste reflecting citizen, i.e. to be guided by our own rationally determined taste and able to substantiate and reflect on judgements of taste. This also applies to the kitchen and when seated around the table. It is important to be able to taste; it is important to be able to substantiate our judgements of taste; and, it is important to be able to reflect on these judgements in the company of others, in the kitchen and around the table.

In other words, it is important to teach children to develop taste competence. Translated into didactics, the question is: How can students learn about, through and for taste? In addition, how should a teacher teach about, through and for taste? This is the main underlying question of the didactics of taste. Having described the history of taste in Part One and a system of taste in Part Two, the rest of Part Three will present the didactics of taste.

What does it mean when we say that a student learns 'about, through and for taste', or that a teacher teaches 'about, through and for taste'? Learning 'about' taste means that taste is the teaching content. For example, the student learns 'about' taste by acquiring knowledge about the five basic flavors or the seven dimensions of taste presented in this book. Learning and teaching 'through' taste means that taste is the form or medium of teaching. For example, the student learns 'through' taste by seasoning the food, meaning that they learn through taste as a medium. Learning or teaching 'for' taste means that taste, taste competences and judgement of taste are the aim of teaching and learning. For example, the student learns 'for' taste when they take part in cooking in order to develop their taste competences, or partake in shared judgement of a meal to develop their judgement of taste.

We will begin by defining what is meant and encompassed by 'didactics', followed by identifying the means and ends of taste education. Finally, we will present an outline of a didactics of taste developed for teachers to help students acquire and develop taste competences, i.e. knowledge and skills regarding taste, and through that develop their personality and become authorities on taste.

DIDACTICS

The teacher: "Come here, my boy, and learn to become wise."
The boy: "What does it mean to become wise?"
The teacher: "Everything that is needed to comprehend what is right, do what is right, say what is right."
The boy: "Who will teach me?"
The teacher: "I will, with God's help."
The boy: "How?"
The teacher: "I will guide you through everything, show you everything, name everything."

The boy: "Look! Here I am! Guide me in God's name!" (Comenius, 1910 [1658]: 2 f.)

This is how Johann Amos Comenius (1592-1670) begins his educational book *Orbis Sensualium Pictus* (*The Visible World in Pictures*) from 1658. The book is an extensive picture book which, through 150 lessons accompanied by German-Latin explanations, guides the student through the natural, social and religious world. The basic principle is that the teacher takes the student by the hand and shows him how the world is structured. As Comenius writes in his theoretical book on didactics, i.e. teaching and learning, *Didactica Magna* from 1628-32 (Comenius, 1960 [1628-32]): "The beginning of cognitions must take the senses as its point of departure at any time."

In the dialogue citation, Comenius presents the classical European definition of didactics: a teacher shows something to a student in order for the student to acquire knowledge and skills and thus become something or someone different. And the starting point of teaching is the senses.

In Comenius' world of tradition, the student's knowledge and skills encompass 'everything', and the student is intended to develop into someone who does the right thing in God's name. Today, the ambitions and aims are different: in a globalized knowledge society, it is not realistic to expect that students can acquire all the knowledge in the world. Rather, they must learn to learn, i.e. acquire basic knowledge and skills that will aid them in learning more. But still, 'showing' takes place, and still, the starting point is the senses, including the sense of taste.

In his book on the educational system of society, Luhmann reformulates these two aims as functions of teaching: the primary function of teaching is to contribute to a student acquiring knowledge and skills; the secondary function is to contribute to a student becoming a person (Luhmann, 2006).

Ergo, any didactics, including the didactics of taste, should describe the aim of teaching (the student becoming something or someone different), process (the teacher showing something) and effect (the student acquiring knowledge and skills). We will return to this below. First, however, the concept of 'didactics' requires further elaboration.

Identifying didactics of taste from a scientific perspective presupposes a distinction between didactic research and didactic reflection on education, in this case in relation to taste: a distinction between didactics as the object of scientific study, and didactics as part of the reflection system of the educational system. Didactics as a concept is mainly used in connection with education and further education, aiming for educators to acquire and develop didactic professionalism (Kruse & Wistoft, 2011). Didactics is the theory of educators. Over recent years, numerous discussions have addressed whether the term 'didactics' should be abandoned at the expense of 'educational theory'; however, in our view, this is quibbling: educational theory is still didactics.

As illustrated with the citation from Comenius, and as the Austrian researcher Stefan Hopmann and others have emphasized, every European cultural tradition from antiquity until today has made didactic considerations (Hopmann, 2007). A common element in these considerations is that didactics can be understood as the art of showing and leading someone to something, which that person cannot necessarily understand on their own. Showing something to someone, or teaching, is still a central part of didactic discussions, but the fundamental idea today is that the person being taught must learn something. The Danish professor emeritus Karsten Schnack, who was one of the leading didactic researchers in Denmark until he retired a few years ago, said that teaching and learning always address something and that teaching is always intentional. The intention is not only for learning to take place, but for a specific form of learning to happen. At the same time, however, he added that teaching can never be expected to be identical with the intention of teaching. Not only must the students learn something; they must also learn to reflect on their own reflections on their surroundings and what they learn. This opens up for moral and ethical reflection (Schnack, 2007: 7), which could, for instance, entail bringing into play the seven dimensions of taste in relation to food choices and in relation to each other, e.g. aesthetic taste versus moral taste: foie gras may taste good until we learn how it is produced. Or pleasant taste versus healthy taste: ice cream may taste good until we learn how fattening it is. In Niklas Luhmann's terms: the students must not only acquire knowledge and skills; they must also develop their self-reflective personality.

Transferring these considerations to a taste-didactic context gives rise to at least three central questions. The first regards didactics in the sense of 'showing' or 'making visible': what are we supposed to show when teaching concerns taste; how can taste be made visible? The second question concerns how students are 'led' to taste so that they not only reflect on taste but also on their own and perhaps others' ways of reflecting on taste? How do they become not only taste competent but also taste reflecting? The third question concerns how teachers are supposed to address the fact that students do not necessarily learn what the teacher expects them to learn? We will return to this below via the concepts of intended and realized learning.

Didactic reflection is today broadly applied to all forms of normative and descriptive problems in connection with teaching and learning processes. Karsten Schnack emphasizes the planning perspective i.e. that the aspects of decision and substantiation regarding the aim (intention) and content of teaching are central and linked to reflections on the form and framework of teaching and learning processes (Schnack, 1992: 61 f.). Three important distinctions can be mentioned in this context:

1. A distinction between teaching and learning. Any teacher knows that teaching and learning are different processes that are not necessarily connected, and one of the central challenges for didactics is to clarify whether and how teaching can result in the learning expected by the teacher. This also applies to taste education. As an educational activity, it is linked to the intention for the students to learn something and to a desire to learn. Without intention and desire, there can be no education. But taste education does not necessarily bring about the expected learning, or any

learning at all, just as (fortunately) it is possible to learn something about taste without being taught.

2. A distinction, on the one hand, between these teaching and learning processes and, on the other, planning them, carrying them out and reflecting on them. Planning can be part of the teaching process, which means that the students take part, at the same time as it is ultimately the teacher's responsibility or the responsibility of the educational institution. For example, the simplified common objectives of the Danish Public Schools, i.e. competence areas with related skills and knowledge objectives, syllabuses, guidelines, learning objectives, challenge task descriptions and learning indicators, contribute to shaping the norms and rules that apply to taking part in teaching. In this sense, class management can be seen as an essential element regarding disciplining with a view to learning, whereas democratic class management concerns the form of self-disciplining that is necessary to learn about the values and value conflicts that unfold when it comes to taste, food and meals.

3. The classical distinction between form and content. Karsten Schnack positions content, aims and intention centrally, at the expense of form or method (Schnack, 1992: 2007). At the beginning of the 19th century, the German educational philosopher Johann Friedrich Herbart (1776-1841) established 'Bildsamkeit' as a central educational concern and invented the concept of 'disciplinary education' as a presupposition for realizing the child's open possibility for Bildung (Herbart, 1964 [1806]), cf. the thorough presentation in Korsgaard, Kristensen & Jensen (2017: 195-198). Since then, part of didactic reflection has concerned the distinction between form and content, or means and ends. Especially in didactics related to Bildung, inspired by Herbart, it has been highlighted that questions about choice of content can only be solved in light of the intention behind the teaching and must, therefore, be made subject to the normative and value-related questions regarding disciplinary education.

Didactics can thus be perceived as reflection on the choice of objectives, content, form, learning aids and media, as well as the substantiation of these choices, considering: who are the students, what are their preconditions and which framework can be established for their active participation, i.e. which physical, social, institutional and cultural context does teaching take place in? To mention a simple example: Food Knowledge teaching does not necessarily have to take place in the school kitchen; it can benefit from being carried out in school gardens or nature (Dyg et al. 2016; Wistoft, 2013; Wistoft et al., 2011).

These decisions manifest themselves as the subject's self-description. Choices and decisions are, according to Stefan Hopmann, one of the two core areas of didactics. The other core area pertains to the understanding of the didactic triangle that describes the interplay between teacher, content and student. In this sense, apart from reflections on process and effect, didactics consists of didactic theory on the aims and ideals of teaching.

BASIC DIDACTIC CONCEPTS

As emphasized above, both teaching and learning are goal-oriented. This is juxtaposed by the fact that all teachers have experienced that teaching often does not fulfil its goals because the students learn something other than what the teacher had expected or intended. Further, all teachers have experienced that students learn outside the formal teaching context. This could be termed 'the didactic dilemma': on the one hand, the concept of 'teaching' is meaningless if it cannot operate with the expectation of defining and reaching goals, i.e. with an idea of causality. On the other hand, the students are free to learn or not learn what they want (Luhmann & Schoor, 1988 [1979]). Obviously, this also applies to taste education and the theory of taste education: didactics of taste. Taste education is goal-orientated. At the same time, any student develops their own taste and opinion about taste.

Naturally, it is important that general didactics, i.e. the theory on the relationship between teaching and learning, and didactics of taste, , provide concepts that reflect this dilemma. In our opinion, these core concepts are 'learning', 'teaching/ education' and 'socialization'.

But what about the German concept of 'Bildung', 'food Bildung' and 'taste Bildung'? Is Bildung not a core concept? The concept of Bildung definitely appears often in the pedagogical debate and has a central position in the history of educational ideas (Korsgaard, Kristensen & Jensen, 2017). In terms of the history of ideas, the concept was introduced as a reaction to the fact that education ceased to orientate itself towards external, societal points of orientation for what a person should be (Luhmann, 2006: 205). Bildung is a result of the interplay between external and individual processes, and the concept of 'Bildsamkeit' was linked to the fundamental, human 'indeterminateness' (Korsgaard, Kristensen & Jensen, 2017: 196). In other words, Bildung becomes a concept that refers both to external formation and self-formation. However, in a didactic context, it is a point of embarrassment to us (Luhmann, 2006: 206), employed when we do not want to, or cannot, express ourselves precisely but rather want to state an opinion. Also, the concept of Bildung often gives rise to problematic associations, for instance indicating that 'more Bildung' creates 'less competence', or that an exaggerated focus on learning objectives and competence weakens the interest in or respect for Bildung.

Like learning, Bildung can be a product or process-related concept. In terms of product, Bildung must be specified according to which results or effects of Bildung are desired in education and upbringing, e.g. the child or student's skills, knowledge and perception of self. Results like these are discussed under OECD headlines such as "21st Century Skills and Competencies" (Dede, 2009), where the concept of Bildung is excluded. In terms of process, Bildung must be specified in accordance with what happens when the child or student is brought up and educated: the child is not only a product of upbringing and education ,it also creates—some might say that it 'builds'—itself. Again, Bildung is seldom specified as a process-related concept. Karsten Schnack and other prominent theorists on Bildung have highlighted that it is impossible to specify the result and process of Bildung, maintaining that Bildung is an ideal (Schnack, 1992, 1998, 2007). In any case, we have more precise concepts at our disposal.

Learning

The first central concept is 'learning', which can be defined as the individual process a student goes through in connection with the epistemological work that is learning. However, learning is not just a process-related but also a product-related concept. We talk about learning as a process or activity related to consciousness. But we also talk about learning as a result, i.e. as a term for the effect of the learning process: we define objectives for learning and achieve outcomes of learning.

In terms of learning as a process, it is important to stress that learning is a consciousness-related and perhaps also bodily process. We will demonstrate below that students' learning is in principle inaccessible for teaching, which is a communicative process. This means that learning can be influenced but not determined by teaching. Learning can be defined as a specific form of externally influenced, goal-oriented self-transformation. What is transformed is meaning, not in the sense of having an 'opinion' but in the sense of something 'making sense'. For example, the teacher may teach the five basic flavors and then say, "Try this ripe tomato. Can you taste umami?" Umami emerges in the consciousness of taste when it makes sense to the student: "Yes, to me this flavor is umami." This learning outcome can subsequently be tested communicatively as the student can investigate whether their opinion of what 'umami' is matches that of the teacher or the other students. The student's learning, as a process of consciousness, can in this sense be expressed indirectly in the teaching situation as a communicative process.

As has been made clear, 'meaning' is a central concept for understanding learning. According to Niklas Luhmann, meaning is a form of self-oriented process that takes place in our consciousness. The consciousness can extract and process information. If we look at the consciousness as a system that operates through self-reference, it must always contribute to transforming its own state of being. In fact, it is this self-reliant transformation process in the consciousness that we denote as learning. The consciousness should not be seen as a simple and open system that can make simple systemic changes through external influence (Luhmann, 2000: 107). The consciousness is a closed system that makes changes to itself through self-transformation.

However, this does not exclude the possibility that the consciousness can be influenced from the outside, for example through teaching. But for the consciousness, an external influence always appears as self-determination i.e. a self-determined influence, and the consciousness must negotiate with itself about the outcome. When the teacher says something, or when something takes place in the teaching communication, the student always needs to put that which is said or takes place in relation to their own prior understanding. The student is bound to relate the teacher's concept of 'umami' to their own knowledge about taste before the concept can make any sense. This is an important point: the student's learning does not take place through a simple process, neither direct transfer of knowledge or mere external influence. Rather, it takes place through what we might term a 'negotiation process' in the consciousness concerning what the student experiences and creates new knowledge about, or learns in other ways, and this production of knowledge and skills will always take place on the basis of what they remember, already know or have experienced.

Taste is a good example in this context, because knowledge and skills are always oriented towards memories and experiences of taste. In order for something to qualify as new meaning (i.e. learning), that which is sensed or tasted must be made the object of a process of meaning. The consciousness is put to work in creating meaning. Information can only become meaning through the interpretation of the consciousness. Any interpretation is dependent on the interpretative schema with which the consciousness operates, and, at the same time, bound to the information provided. How does the new flavor come across compared to pre-existing memories and experiences of taste? Or how can meaning be ascribed to a new concept of taste in relation to the concepts of taste already established? An interpretation is a conscious selection of meaning within a scope of possibilities suggested and perceived as relevant by the consciousness itself. However, interpretation and formation of meaning always takes place in relation to information in the environment. Meaning always refers to other meaning. The consciousness can never experience or act independently of meaning (Luhmann, 2000: 101). This entails that we cannot 'escape' meaning. Even that which has no meaning can only be experienced through meaning.

In terms of learning as an effect, we can distinguish between intended and realized learning. Intended learning encompasses objectives built on ideals, ambitions or expectations, i.e. the aims that a student or teacher has for a specific educational activity in relation to expected learning. This can be juxtaposed with realized learning, which denotes a student's actual outcome of a specific educational activity. Whereas intended learning, from the teacher's perspective, is a generalized ambition linked to the communication taking place during the educational activity, realized learning is an individual and often very different experience that can be more or less close to the intended learning. However, intended learning is not just the teacher's domain. The students' intended learning, as a sign of what they expect to learn, is also an important factor. Their perception of the characteristics of the learning process should not be viewed as detached from realized learning.

Non-intended Learning

Any educator is familiar with the phenomenon that students not only acquire opinions, knowledge and skills through teaching, i.e. in the form of intended learning, but also through various other influences. This is certainly the case in taste education: the student's taste is not only, and probably not mainly, a result of taste education but also of what happens in their family, among friends and in other social, i.e. communicative, contexts.

This means that the didactic taste repertoire has to distinguish between learning that is intended and to some extent stimulated by teaching, and teaching that comes about more unnoticed, i.e. is non-intended. This form of learning can, as suggested by Qvortrup and Keiding, be termed 'development' (Qvortrup & Keiding, 2017: 49 f.). In other words, 'development' is a term for what others call informal or non-formalized learning and we call non-intended learning.

We can exemplify the difference between learning and development in the following way: one of the aims of taste education is for the students to understand and use the five basic flavors in seasoning the dishes they cook together (Qvortrup & Keiding, 2017: 50). This understanding, i.e. whether that the realized learning matches the intended learning, can be documented via the finished dish and the students' presentation and qualification of it. Whether the students use the five basic flavors correctly in presenting the dish is testimony to their learning, and it will tell the teacher whether the realized learning matches the intended learning. At the same time, the students will naturally draw on all the experiences and preferences of taste they have gathered from other contexts, i.e. outside the teaching situation, and these will influence the seasoning, the finished dish and their reflection on it. The teacher can view all this as signs of non-intended yet realized learning.

Teaching and Education

The third central concept is 'teaching'. Teaching denotes a communicative situation in which an educational activity takes place. Teaching is not an inner experience but a communicative situation. What characterizes teaching, compared to other forms of communication, is that it is goal-oriented. Teaching is intentional communication, and the intention is the students' learning outcome. The intention is for the students to learn, and for them to learn something specific rather than something altogether different.

At the same time, we have already established that teaching cannot connect directly but only indirectly with learning. In order to express this indirect link between teaching and learning, we use the term 'structural link' with reference to Luhmann (Luhmann, 2000). By way of structural links, teaching can stimulate students' learning because the concepts, relations and activities of teaching can function as a structure for consciousness-related learning. This means that teaching can take place without learning, i.e. when the intended learning does not become realized learning. At the same time, we cannot rule out that the teaching stimulates some other form of learning than that intended. The teacher touches upon a topic in the teaching that makes the students think about something completely different.

A concept that is related to teaching is 'education': a term for the overall framework or organization in which the teaching takes place, and through which the teaching must be directed and legitimized, both in a subject-related and an ideological perspective. The function of the educational system is to contribute to specific intentional learning in contrast to all the non-intentional learning (development) that also takes place. Overall teaching objectives are established through legislation and administrative activities, and these, in turn, are implemented as a number of specific objectives. As described in regard to the subject of Food Knowledge and suggested in this book, the overall objective of the subject is to stimulate the student in developing into a taste competent person, whereas the specific objectives are for the student to develop a number of taste competences, i.e. taste-related and taste-oriented knowledge and skills.

Learning that can be described in relation to a specific education that includes taste education is learning that is linked to taste in the course modules and can have a number of learning intentions. The learning intentions are always guided by specific rules that reflect the basic educational-ideological ideas on the background of which specific forms of meaning, skill and knowledge are given priority. It is these sets of values, basic ideas and learning practices that are employed in taste education.

Socialization

As mentioned above, we need to distinguish between two processes in the consciousness: the intentional and the non-intentional. Accordingly, we can distinguish between two systems of communication that both stimulate learning and development but are different by being goal-oriented versus non-goal-oriented. The goal-oriented communication that stimulates learning is called teaching. This is a form of communication that is learning intentional. We suggest the term socialization to denote the non-goal-oriented form of communication that nevertheless stimulates learning. This form of communication is not learning intentional.

Both teaching/education and socialization are activities that shape the opportunities and lives of individuals. The difference is related to the intentional aim. Whereas teaching and education are organized around intended changes, socialization functions through unnoticed and concomitant transformations (Qvortrup & Keiding, 2017: 49). One example is the meal habits in families. When the student learns about food culture and well-being in connection with communal meals in school, at the same time as being part of a family that does not have time to eat breakfast or dinner together, the student's own socialization is in opposition to the teaching, and, thereby, the non-intended learning of the socialization is in opposition to the intended learning of the teaching.

Learning, Teaching/Education and Socialization: Summary

To sum up, and with reference to taste education, the concepts of 'learning', 'teaching/ education' and 'socialization' can be exemplified as follows. The students take part in an outdoor teaching module through the program 'Gardens to Bellies', where they grow and harvest their own vegetables and forage for wild herbs in the woods. They prepare these with other ingredients and cook the meal over open fire in the outdoor kitchen. Together, they experiment with the food and subsequently serve it to each other and eat it together.

During the entire project, teaching is understood as a communicative event arranged with certain objectives. The teaching is communication with learning intentions. The learning intentions and methods of the teaching are inspired and informed by the goal descriptions of the educational system.

Simultaneously, however, socialization takes place. The students communicate with each other and influence each other's activities and preferences. They might be absorbed in making purple pancakes from blue potatoes because they have never seen or tasted anything like that before; they may turn their noses up at the herbs they gather in the woods because the teacher has said that they are special; or they may opt for taste criteria that do not stem from the school garden teaching but from experiences acquired among friends or family.

The effect of the project is learning. The learning intention of the teaching results in realized learning, i.e. learning that is a result of the teaching module, even if it does not match exactly what the teacher had expected or hoped for. The teacher cannot observe the realized learning directly but only indirectly in the way it is manifested through the students' actions and communication.

But the effect of the project is also non-intended learning: a vast number of activities take place during the module that are not intended and are affected by non-planned activities. One student is influenced by another; a community of taste occurs which may be in opposition to the teacher's taste ideals; collaborative competences are developed, which the teacher has not planned but notices with satisfaction. The students develop themselves and each other through the project and its many socialization processes.

Visible Learning

Interpreting teaching and learning in the light of systems theory requires that a number of conditions are kept separate. As demonstrated above, learning can be described as self-created self-transformation (Qvortrup, 2004), understood as the mental system's transformation of its own competences, i.e. knowledge and skills. Teaching can be described as a specific form of goal-oriented communication. Therefore, teaching and learning are two independent processes that take place in two different and mutually independent systems: the social (communication) and the mental (consciousness). This is not to say that they are completely unrelated. On the contrary, they may become mutually dependent though structural links. Teaching can provide concepts and relations for the consciousness to work with, whereas the consciousness can provide an understanding of concepts and relations for communication to work with.

Because teaching is oriented towards desired learning, but at the same time cannot causally affect or determine the processes and structures of mental systems, teaching must resort to the socially accessible signs of learning. In other words, teaching can ascribe learning to students when they show signs of it. In order for signs of learning to become part of the didactic reflection, some illustrative examples are needed.

When teaching ascribes skills and knowledge to students, we talk about a learning outcome. The point here is that a learning outcome can be a result of the teaching, the student's own activity or something other (e.g. non-teaching social activities such as play, work, media, games, etc.). A learning outcome in regard to taste does not have to be the result of taste education; it can just as well be the result of the student's memories and other experiences of taste. This is most often the case, given that taste is linked to taste experiences in the form of memories of taste and taste experiences in the form of tasting in the social sphere.

The question of effect – how taste education works – can thus be interpreted as a question of how the teaching achieves the desired learning result or outcome. The criteria for judging the success of taste education must be described through didactic reflection. Such a description of the criteria for success can be used to reduce the complexity of taste education and, thereby, pave the way for the desired learning outcomes. The didactic reflections are not insubstantial; for example, there is a vast difference between whether the aim is a) to teach the student to taste (everything); b) to provide the student with knowledge about, and the ability to employ, the five basic flavors; c) to teach the student to season food; d) to teach the student to experiment with taste in their own dishes; or, e) to teach the student to use taste to make informed food choices. The first two aims are often linked to ideas of 'the good taste', 'the right seasoning' and 'good food or meals'. The last two aims are linked to ideas of using one's own senses and acquiring skills and knowledge about taste, i.e. taste competence.

Based on this, we can use the New Zealand researcher John Hattie's famous and contested concept 'visible learning'. The main benefit of Hattie's research is not that we can list learning effects. Rather, it is central for the individual teacher that they can make learning visible in teaching communication in the form of signs of learning, because this is a crucial precondition for realizing the learning effects of the teaching. The inspiration behind this approach is, among other works, Hattie's meta-study *Visible Learning* (Hattie, 2009), where one of the points is that simple and precise learning objectives should continuously be presented to the students in order to make the aim of the teaching visible. This applies to learning objectives for whole teaching modules but also, and importantly, to learning objectives for each lesson. The intention is to provide the students with a clear picture of what they are supposed to learn, and to make them conscious about their own learning process through continuous feedback. This approach requires that the teacher reflects on which signs of learning can be observed and on how to formulate the learning objectives in a way that makes it visible to both the students and the teacher themselves whether they have been reached (Hattie, 2009: 173-178, 246-247). What happens is that the student's learning, which is in principle invisible to the teacher, is made visible through communicatively accessible signs of learning.

Didactics of Taste as Such

Having described the central didactic concepts and exemplified them through the didactics of taste, we will now turn to outlining our didactics of taste. We will begin by briefly describing the aims, effects and processes of taste education. This will be followed by three main sections. The first section concerns how taste must be made the crux of didactics of taste and taste education. We have already shown this in a historical (Part One) and systematic (Part Two) perspective. Here, in Part Three, we demonstrate that it should also take place didactically, not least for the simple reason that it stimulates the students' learning expectations. The second section concerns the fundamental structure of the didactics of taste. The third section concerns the development of the students as authorities on taste.

Means and Ends of Teaching

As described in the didactic tradition, and as reformulated by Luhmann (2006), teaching has two aims: that the student acquires knowledge and skills, and that the student becomes a person. If we move from general didactics to didactics of taste, this means that the two aims of taste education are:

- The taste competent student: the student should acquire knowledge and skills related to taste

- The taste confident student: the student should develop taste authority, i.e. become an authority on taste

Effects and Processes of Teaching

It is common to distinguish between the aims and effects of teaching. It is also, like in the present book, an option to distinguish between intended and realized learning; in that case, 'effect' is a term for realized learning. We use 'processes' to indicate that which takes place in and around teaching situations. Teaching is intentional in the sense that the teacher works towards reaching specific objectives, i.e. turning intended learning into realized learning. We use 'education' to indicate the framework around teaching in school and generally in educational institutions in society. However, students do not only learn from teaching but also from other social contexts which they are part of among friends and family. The difference is that friends and family do not usually have specific learning intentions related to the framework and activities they create. The influential process that takes place here is non-intentional, and we call it 'socialization'.

- Effects: realized learning

- Processes: teaching, education and socialization

This distinction between effects and processes also encompasses a distinction between processes in the students' consciousness (intended and non-intended learning) and social processes that exist as communication (teaching and socialization). A vital consequence of this distinction is that a teacher can never 'create' or 'produce' learning, but only, through the teaching communication, contribute to students acquiring knowledge and skills through self-referential cognitive processes.

Focusing on Taste

This part about the didactics of taste mainly concerns 'taste competences' and 'taste authority'. But before arriving at these concepts, we will briefly qualify why taste should be made the focus of food, meal and Food Knowledge teaching. In Part One, the argument was historical: reading children's cookbooks from 1971-2016 demonstrates how taste has become central. In Part Two, the argument was systematic: taste 'as such', or taste as a quality, is central to the many dimensions of taste. In this part, the argument is didactic. Looking into Food Knowledge teaching will reveal that the students learn more, or at least have higher expectations of learning, if taste is the focus.

New research demonstrates correlations between students' learning expectations and different didactic elements in Home Economics (Christensen & Wistoft, 2016). The research also demonstrates a positive correlation between the students' learning expectations and general didactic elements such as participation, motivation, innovation and collaboration. This is not groundbreaking; much didactic research has arrived at the same conclusion over time. The correlation between taste and expected learning, on the other hand, is a far less explored area, and the new research mentioned (cf. Christensen & Wistoft, 2016) indicates that the experience of working with taste in the subject of Food Knowledge may not only have a similar effect but an even larger one than the general didactic elements such as student participation and innovation. The learning intentions are always guided by specific sets of values that reflect basic educational or ideological ideas, and these basic ideas serve to prioritize specific forms of cognition, skill and knowledge. These sets of values and basic ideas, and the learning practices employed in taste education during Home Economics lessons, are central in the research.

Students' learning expectations can be seen as a form of self-reported learning. Such data can always be criticized due to the difference between the self-reported, subjective assessment of own learning and realized learning in a more 'objective' perspective. Also, there can be much variation in relation to different students' subjective perceptions of what it means to have learned something. However, the research design was developed with a starting point in systems theory, where the basic idea of subject/object is replaced by the basic idea of system/ environment (Luhmann, 2000). In conjunction with the perspective of visible learning and the limitations it entails (Luhmann, 2006: 189), self-reporting is a method to make the students communicate about their own learning. Studies have shown that self-reported learning generally does not deviate significantly from realized learning. As

John Hattie writes: "Students are very adept at knowing how to rate their performance" (Hattie, 2009: 31).

The Danish researcher in food education, Jacob Christensen's, PhD thesis *A Scientific Didactic Perspective on the School Subject Food Knowledge* with the Danish Home Economics Championship as Field of Research takes into account the factors of gender and social class, showing that the effect of working with taste in the subject of Food Knowledge is no longer the privilege of specific groups of students but rather a didactic element that all students can benefit from in achieving learning objectives (Christensen, 2017). Further, the research shows that the learning effect is not significantly increased by a focus on sensed taste, for example the five basic flavors. Knowledge and teaching focusing on this aspect only does not increase the students' learning expectations, whereas they can be affected positively by nuanced and varied taste teaching, where they are inspired to experiment with taste, share taste experiences, create new dishes on the basis of taste, and make and discuss judgements of taste (Christensen, 2017).

This might come across as obvious because taste is inevitable when human beings engage with food and meals. However, as seen in the historical part, it is not at all obvious in a historical perspective. Focus has been on many other factors: cleanliness, hygiene, the ability to follow recipes by the letter, political understanding of organic farming, etc. Taste only recently became a focal point. But even if it were obvious, it is important to emphasize that the students appear to have different experiences of the degree to which they have addressed the topic of taste. Teachers give different priorities to taste as an active element of Food Knowledge teaching. The cited research shows that when, for example, participation and innovation are prioritized, there is a risk of teaching and work with taste being pushed into the background. If this is the case, it will result in the students not benefitting from the positive effect brought about by working with taste. The point is that Home Economics education that prioritizes taste as both experiment and content element has a significantly positive effect on the students' own expectations of learning (Christensen & Wistoft, 2016).

Food Knowledge

The ideal of taste as a focal point has been realized in the subject of Food Knowledge, which is one of the two new subjects introduced in the 2014 Danish school reform. Food Knowledge replaced the former subject of Home Economics, not just as a 'modernization' but as an entirely new subject profile with new areas of competence and new objectives such as taste, sensitivity, sustainability, climate, food waste, etc.

Food Knowledge is guided by learning objectives, just like the other subjects included in the reform, and the subject adheres to the general ideas of the reform regarding varied and practice-oriented teaching, supportive teaching, linguistic development, IT and media, and innovation and entrepreneurship. Food Knowledge is both a practical and theoretical subject in that it combines the practical craft of cooking with experiences and knowledge about food and cooking, taste, health, meals, food sources and consumption. As described in the goal description, the subject offers varied learning modules where the students acquire practical knowledge and skills through which they develop competences that make them capable of making critically qualified food choices (EMU. DK/modul/madkundskab-fælles-mål-læseplan-og-vejledning).

The practical aspect mainly concerns cooking, and not just according to specific recipes. The subject facilitates experiments with known and unknown foods and allows the students to develop new recipes and dishes. Therefore, Food Knowledge focuses on taste and other sensory impressions that, in combination with knowledge, lay the foundation for the ability to make critically qualified food choices and judge the quality of food and meals.

In Food Knowledge, the students work with four areas of competence: 1) Food and Health; 2) Food Awareness; 3) Cooking; and 4) Meal and Food Cultures. All four areas of competence should not necessarily be included in every course module but be selected with a view to the concrete teaching topics and modules.

Food Knowledge offers the opportunity for the students to work with their senses and experiences, and to experiment, create and communicate in relation to food and meals. The students train their new skills and knowledge through activities that activate motor skills, cognition and perception. Food knowledge entails different opportunities for strengthening the students' learning and cognition. Many things indicate that the single most important factor for students learning something new is that they can relate it to something they already know (Kruse, 2007). Therefore, it is very important for learning that the students' skills and prior experiences are activated during teaching. For the same reason, the teaching guide encourages teaching that takes into account both the students' existing skills and the formal subject requirements according to the syllabus.

How is taste included as a part of Food Knowledge at a concrete level? As mentioned above, the subject has four core areas: 1) Food and health; 2) Food awareness; 3) Cooking; and 4) Meal and food cultures. Taste plays an important part, especially in the last three.

Competence area 3, Cooking, is the largest competence area. Here, the students should, for instance, experiment with ingredients. Based on an understanding of the physical-chemical reaction of the ingredients when they are cooked separately, the students should compose new dishes and experiment with new combinations of ingredients, focusing on consistency, taste and smell, and with their knowledge about the physical-chemical properties of the food. On a so-called elective course, the students can move beyond this to work with combinations of ingredients in relation to new gastronomic trends and scientific molecular gastronomy. Taste is a recurring element in all the experimental teaching activities.

In competence area 2, Food Awareness, taste plays a similarly central role. The competence objective is for the student to become able to make qualified food choices in regard to quality, taste and sustainability. The syllabus states that the students should work with the physical-chemical properties, uses and taste of food. This knowledge should be transferred to dishes in which they continue working with taste. The students should work with qualitative criteria and conditions for production, so that they become able to judge the quality of industrially produced foods. Teaching should focus on the taste-related aesthetic properties of food by experimenting with tastes, basic methods and seasoning and by discussing experiences.

Competence area 4, Meal and food cultures, is also full of taste. The pleasure of taking part in a delicious communal meal is prioritized highly in the teaching, which emphasizes well-being, solidarity, diversity and taste. The syllabus states that the students should work with the pleasure of food and quality of life through their own taste experiences, as well as their understanding of others' experiences. The teaching guide accentuates the importance of teaching that creates a suitable environment for experiencing fellowship, responsibility and care in relation to the meals. This can partly be ensured by prioritizing the quality, including the taste, of the food. By having the students serve different dishes, focus is directed at the importance for the taste and the meal of food arrangement, ambience and company.

Meal culture should focus on taste differences between cultures and places, and how different tastes in food and meal cultures develop and mutually influence each other (Højlund, 2015). Taste in this context includes food and meals in a social, multicultural and historical perspective. 'Culture' cannot be understood as an unambiguous concept. Rather, the culture of food and meals should be understood as a system of rules and conventions for when, what and with whom we eat. Cultural norms also refer to what is 'good' and 'bad' in connection with taste. Taste preferences differ, for example between countries, regions, local communities, social groups, age groups and genders. Taste preferences contribute to marking communities within the sociality in question and demarcating them (Bourdieu, 1979; Leer & Wistoft, 2015). In this sense, taste is conceived of as being closely related to human identity.

In regard to identity and taste preferences, it becomes pivotal to the teaching that the students are given the opportunity to represent their different food and meal cultures. The guidelines encourage student presentations and discussions of own taste preferences and those of others. Teaching should take into account the students' different ways of eating and their meal norms, including taste preferences. The intention is to give students the opportunity to work with food and meals with a focus on how taste preferences, values, norms, habits and traditions are created through human intercourse, in relation to different lifestyles and living conditions. By including their own memories and experiences of taste, the students should compare food and meal cultures from different times and places.

Taste in the subject of Food Knowledge is thus not only linked to cooking and food awareness but also to culture and identity, and it cannot be taken for granted. Teaching should favor a view of taste that can be modelled or transformed as a result of the influences of environment and individual memories, experiences and social (inter)action.

Already in 2014, when Food Knowledge was introduced as a new subject in connection with the Danish school reform, the book *Food Knowledge* (Carlsen & Pedersen, 2014) was published. The target group was teachers of Food Knowledge, and the aim was to provide a foundation for teaching the subject. The book provides knowledge about food, nutrition, health and hygiene, as well as contributing to teaching material design, etc. Helle Brønnum Carlsen subsequently published the book *Food Knowledge Didactics* with the subtitle *Between Subject and Didactics*. The book presents many of the factors that teachers of Food Knowledge need to consider in order to plan good and meaningful teaching. Didactic questions about what should be taught in Food Knowledge, and how and why, are supported in the book by descriptions of different views of subjects, human beings and learning (Carlsen, 2017). In comparison to the present book, however, both books employ a different view on taste and didactics, and their scope is narrower.

BASIC TASTE DIDACTIC STRUCTURE

The above sections have summarized the basic elements of the didactic tradition, presenting the learning objectives and preconditions for taste education. They have documented that there are solid didactic reasons for making taste a central element when it comes to teaching food and meals. It simply heightens the students' learning expectations, which is one of the decisive preconditions for a high learning outcome. Finally, they have established that taste was in fact given center stage when the subject of Food Knowledge was introduced in 2014. With this in mind, we will now describe a fundamental structure for the didactics of taste in the form of three overall categories with associated subcategories.

The first category concerns the self-description of taste education, which includes the basic didactic assumptions, theories, knowledge and ideals, and also the teaching program that constitutes the framework, including descriptions of:

a) Aim, i.e. the intention, qualification and value-orientation of taste education, and thereby the criteria for determining objectives for students' learning in the form of expected learning outcomes, including visible signs of learning. Here, it is important that both the aim – in this connection the student as an authority on taste and, especially, the learning objectives – are designed to make it visible to both students and teachers whether they have been reached.

b) The selection, structuring and order of content in a subject-related context. What we work with and when. It is here in particular that our system of taste, featuring the seven dimensions of taste, becomes central, providing an answer to the question of 'what': what is taught when teaching revolves around taste? Which dimensions are encompassed by taste? How should teaching be structured? The system of taste is an aid in ordering and structuring the content. The teaching examples described as part of each dimension of taste provide suggestions for teaching. Naturally, content should be selected and structured in accordance with the aim: the student as an authority on taste.

c) The form and method of taste education: how can learning outcomes or effects become visible through the teaching design, including use of learning aids, which, in taste education, can be materials, products or taste experiences? Taste education can operate with a broad selection of concrete learning aids, e.g. ingredients, finished food products, kitchen utensils, textbooks, cookbooks, recipes, food blogs, films, food commercials, food and health debate programs, etc. Teaching aids also include the students' own products in the form of recipes and instructions, own videos and drawings, etc. Prose on food and taste can also be included, as well as art and other aesthetic learning aids that have food as a motif. Meal spaces and concrete materials used when setting the scene for meals (plates, cutlery, drinking glasses, tablecloths, candles, etc.) are also learning aids. The same applies to digital learning aids such as food blogs, web-based programs for dietary or nutritional calculation, reference works on food and meals on the Internet, demo videos, etc. School gardens that facilitate growing vegetables and cooking outside can also be viewed as learning aids.

d) Didactic management, which we understand as teaching management that continuously aims to stabilize the expected objectives, processes and effects of teaching through planning and adjustment. According to the German sociologist Dirk Baecker, didactic management contributes to the success of teaching in conjunction with interpretation of the framework (Baecker, 2006). This framework concerns the physical environment, the teaching space and the individual student, as well as the societal opportunities presented by economy, politics, rules, production conditions, science, etc. At the personal level, it concerns who the students and the teachers are. At the societal level, it concerns, among other things, how education manages the economic, political, legal, occupational and scientific preconditions that pertain to the specific education. Didactic management is about the physical environment and should be understood in relation to the framework conditions and framework factors of education (Luhmann, 2006; Lindblad & Sahlström, 1999), and particularly of taste education. Here, we distinguish between the external framework, which has been established in and around the individual education, and the internal framework, which can be viewed as independently chosen and thereby part of the possibility of change bestowed upon the educational institutions. The independently chosen framework is shaped through decisions pertaining to the roles of teachers and students, and the plans for learning and management of the core tasks of education: in this case, who (teachers and students) is doing what (working with taste), where (in the teaching space, e.g. a kitchen), and when (at what times).

The second category concerns realized taste education and learning, including subject-specific, social and temporal dimensions:

a) The students' motivation, background and preconditions for taking part in taste education. Are the students school pupils, and if so, what are their subject-related and social preconditions? What year are we talking about? Have they opted for the subject where taste education is included? Or, are the students trainee chefs, and in that case, what is their background and preconditions? What characterizes their motivation, and how do they engage in taste education? What would they like to learn, and how do they prepare for learning? The content, the system of taste with its seven dimensions of taste, can also influence the students' involvement. Some of the dimensions might be of specific interest to some students, while others might be outside their scope of interest. Teaching should be carried out in a way that pays heed to the students' motivation, background and preconditions for learning, which is not to say that it should be arranged only according to their interests. But, as exemplified above, allowing the students to take part in planning how they work with the dimensions of taste on the basis of their competences works as a motivational factor.

b) The sets of values (norms) and basic ideas as they are expressed in the concrete learning practices during teaching. This concerns both the knowledge and the norms that apply to taste education, and thereby also the arguments, ideas and theories that the teacher employs in relation to choice of content, form and method, in addition to didactic management. What is given weight in the teaching situation and why? How are values and arguments made visible to the students, and how can they be adjusted according to the students' preconditions for learning? Are some of the seven dimensions of taste more important than others? And if this is the case, then why? We could refer to this as reflected clarification of values towards the students in relation to concrete teaching. This obviously includes the question of what evidence of values and basic ideas becomes visible to the students through teaching.

c) The internal and external opportunities entailed in taste education, including the physical, ideological, economic and political conditions. How can taste education be carried out in practice? Which potentials and limitations are there for teaching? Which organizational conditions and decisions pertain to the concrete teaching of taste? Again, we distinguish between the educational organization outside teaching and the internal organization of teaching, which is coordinated via decisions about teaching activities in time and space, and guides the expected roles in the teaching. For example, there is a difference between teaching the subject of Food Knowledge in school, on occupational college degrees or as part of teacher training.

d) The realization and adjustment of teaching in light of the students' learning expectations and visible signs of learning, including teacher/ student roles. As mentioned earlier, the students' learning expectations can be seen as a form of self-reported learning. Nuanced taste education, where the students are given the opportunity to experiment with taste, share taste experiences, create new dishes on the basis of taste and discuss their judgements of taste, increases the likeliness of learning (Christensen & Wistoft, 2016). Therefore, it is important to make adjustments in accordance with the students' learning expectations, indicating that they are perceived as authorities on, and competent learners of, taste. We will return to taste authority. The learning assessment competence is inextricably linked with the students' preconditions for learning. Nevertheless, it is important that teachers make their teaching competence available to an adjustment of roles if necessary. For instance, there is not much point in a teaching perspective where the teacher assumes the role as expert of taste, unless the expertise is consistent with didactic professionalism, which we will return to below. On the other hand, there is not much point, either, in students assuming the role as fuzzy or dismissive in relation to taste, unless they can justify it through reflected judgements of taste or authority of taste, as we call it. We will return to this as well. Here, signs of learning are central. The realization of learning cannot be included in reflection if it cannot be observed.

The third taste didactic category concerns what we term didactic professionalism, including teachers' clarification of their own taste values, taste preferences and attitudes towards taste:

a) Clarification of knowledge and values is part of the teaching competence related to didactic professionalism. Recent sociological and pedagogical research shows that modern professions are characterized by a high level of professionalism, which, according to the American sociologist Robert K. Merton (Merton, 1982, cf. also Qvortrup, 2016), includes three basic values. The first is 'knowing', which is related to systematic knowledge and specialized thinking. 'Knowing' entails that the profession refers to research-based theoretical and empirical knowledge unknown to the general population. The second value is 'doing', which, firstly, entails that the profession is capable of solving complex tasks by using technical skills and practical competences and, secondly, that representatives of the profession can account for methods used in solving the tasks. This means that the profession can be expected to use theoretical knowledge to solve practical problems. The third value is 'helping', which entails that the 'knowing' and 'doing' of the professionals are combined to realize the ideals of the profession. Transferred to the context of taste education, it means that the teachers need extensive knowledge about taste and taste education; practical experience with taste education; and professionally founded attitudes towards taste and judgements of taste. Put succinctly, they need to exercise professional taste-didactic power of judgement.

b) Therefore, the individual teacher's approach to taste is not insignificant. The teacher's choice of knowledge (for example, the system of taste with the seven dimensions of taste), teaching structure, form and method are always influenced by values. Values are not only social; some belong in the consciousness of the individual teacher and are therefore individual. This specifically pertains to taste preferences because they are always dependent on taste experiences as they take place in the mental system or consciousness. Of course, they can be shared communicatively (Wistoft, 2009); when this happens during taste education, it is the teacher's own taste preferences and approaches that are expressed.

c) The teacher's clarification of the weighting of content, i.e. communicated values, might be the crucial part of taste education. Choice and weighting of some or all of the seven dimensions of taste in our system of taste will reflect the teacher's own attitudes to taste, taste preferences and judgements of taste. Therefore, it is important that they are clarified to avoid the teaching becoming 'private', based on invisible knowledge and values. The teacher's attitudes should be visible and communicated through their dimensions and choices of taste, inviting debate with the students.

Fundamental Issues

The above-mentioned three categories encompass the fundamental issues of didactics, which we can be formulated in the following questions: What constitutes taste education as a specific social activity? How can taste education further the students' attention and involvement? Which factors can make the work with taste valuable and meaningful for the students? How can the students' own taste experiences and taste preferences be included in the teaching? What kind of teaching climate furthers the students' willingness to taste, wonder, experiment and judge their choices of food? Why is this important? The answer: because food and meals are not insignificant, and because taste is both an individual taste experience and the result of social interaction. Taste is both individual and social.

Didactics of taste that reflects awareness, development of competence and critical food choices does not take a point of departure in management and control. Our suggested didactics of taste is thus a response to the ambition of managing or controlling children and young people's taste. Children and young people are no different to independent adult individuals, each with their own integrity of which taste is an important part. Integrity concerns how they experience the sense and quality of staying honest and true to the motives behind their own actions. Integrity of taste is connected to the quality of their own taste preferences. The students should expand their consciousness (learning) about their own taste and that of others. Teaching should leave room for the students to experience, act out and appreciate this new consciousness. This didactics of taste requires that the goal is the student as an authority on taste, i.e. that the student acquires new knowledge about taste and new skills in relation to tasting and judging their own taste and that of others.

The Taste Competent Student

Having described the basic didactic and taste didactic concepts, and outlined a basic structure for a didactics of taste, the two concluding sections will address the aims of taste education, i.e. the didactic reflection on objectives. What should the students know and be capable of, and what should they become? The former question concerns the student as taste competent; the latter concerns the student as an authority on taste.

The question of taste competence can be divided into four parts: 1) Should the students be included or involved? 2) How can the students acquire the desired taste habits and competence? 3) Is it only the students that should learn from taste education? 4) How can education and socialization be combined?

1. Should the students be included or involved? When it comes to students taking part in something, for example something that promotes health, which can be taught through cooking with the aim of learning about healthy food, 'inclusion' is not enough because inclusion is always inclusion into something that is already decided or established by someone other than the students. Often, adults, parents or teachers have determined the aims or conceived the idea. Inclusion does not give the students enough joint ownership because they have not contributed to developing the idea or setting the agenda for what they are supposed to learn about which healthy dish to learn to cook and how. This means that we need to take a step up the ladder of participation: the term 'involvement' is better suited because it means that the students are allowed to be co-creators and thereby claim mental co-ownership of what should be made and learned. 'To involve' comes from the Latin for 'envelop'. According to Oxford Online Dictionaries, 'to involve' can mean "Cause to participate in an activity or situation", i.e. to take an active part in something. It is important that the students take an active part in charting the course rather than simply being led in a direction dictated by others. When they contribute to the choice of topic or dish, or, even better, create the dish through taste, there is a better chance that they will become engaged, which is connected to their increased desire to learn. In other words, there is a better chance that intended learning about healthy food becomes realized learning.

2. How can the students acquire the desired taste habits and competence? Neither habits nor competence can be acquired from others. For years, scientific research has pointed out that children carry their habits, whether food, meal, movement or other health or risk-related habits, with them into

adult life, which serves as an argument for early intervention in children's lives to ensure good, healthy habits in adult life. There is nothing wrong with this argument, except that the idea of adults giving habits or competences to children is incongruent with our knowledge about learning and development of competences. As described, we cannot produce learning for others; learning takes place in the consciousness of the individual student and others can only stimulate it or set up a framework for that which happens either intentionally through teaching or non-intentionally through socialization. We have not addressed the concept of 'habits' until now, because we believe that the concept of 'competence' has served to create an understanding of the fact that the idea of 'giving learning' to someone needs to be replaced by the idea of learning as a development in the consciousness of the individual student. The same applies to habits. We cannot 'create' good habits for others, but we can create a framework and conditions that make it likely that others can develop good habits for themselves.

3. Is it only the students that should learn from taste education? When it comes to children's food and meals, the common understanding is that adults should teach children something, for example by ensuring that the children taste the food that is served. This understanding is far too one-sided. A learning process usually involves a teacher, but it is not only the students who have the opportunity to learn. The teacher also always has the opportunity to open their consciousness to the students' learning and thus learn themselves. Let us look at a concrete example: a packed lunch is not only a source of energy; to a parent, it should be conceived as something far more significant. The packed lunch can present an opportunity to involve the child in choosing, tasting and deciding what they would like; further, if adults and children prepare packed lunches together, it is both a chance to spend enjoyable time together and a chance for the adult to learn something about the child's taste. Preparing packed lunches together can be a learning process for the child because it can realize the adult's intention of teaching the child about ingredients and flavors. But the collaboration can also teach the parent about their child's taste. Similarly, teaching that revolves around taste can be seen as an opportunity for the teacher to learn from the students' taste experiences and judgements of taste.

4. How can education and socialization be combined? Because it is not only teaching, with its intended learning, but also socialization that contributes to developing students' awareness of food and taste, we cannot settle for thinking in terms of teaching, guidance and other educational activities. Taste competence is just as much developed through socialization, which means that teachers cannot only think in terms of teaching and learning plans. Taste experiences take place in the students' consciousness with

reference to what they taste. However, as described (with reference to Kant), the fact that they taste individually is not interesting in itself. Taste experiences must be shared to become interesting and thereby contribute to development. Taste needs to be made communicatively accessible, i.e. part of and shared in community, and in that sense be made an object for development of taste competences and judgements of taste. Furthermore, it is Kant's point that judgements of taste motivate a sense of community, which is a framework for socialization. This point entails two things: first, taste competence is only created through learning but also through socialization; second, judgements of taste call for a sense of community, which in itself is significant if the communal is not seen as a given. Following one's judgements of taste results in becoming an authority on taste (see the next section).

These four points identify at least some of the preconditions for students acquiring and developing taste competence, i.e. knowledge and skills in relation to taste. They need to know something about taste and how to realize taste, not only in a sensory perspective but also through the other dimensions of taste introduced in Part Two. Further, they need to develop taste skills, i.e. practical skills to transfer their knowledge into creating food and meals, or, vice versa, to transfer skills into knowledge about taste.

All this constitutes a necessary, albeit not in itself sufficient, part of taste education. Competence is necessary but not enough, because knowledge and skills without general ideals are blind, just like general ideals are void if they are not filled up and realized by means of extensive knowledge and strong skills (Qvortrup & Qvortrup, 2013). This dilemma is far too often portrayed as a zero-sum game: competences are developed at the expense of what is called general education. We view things differently: without taste competence, personal taste authority is an empty concept, and without personal taste authority, taste competence is aimless. On this basis, we will now turn to the final section of the book about how students can develop into authorities on taste.

The Taste Autonomous Person

In addition to contributing to the students acquiring taste competences, the second overall aim of a didactics of taste, as emphasized above inspired by Kant, is to teach students how to develop taste authority. The students should become authorities on taste. They should develop themselves into taste autonomous persons.

What does that entail? This question can be addressed through a clarification of the knowledge forms and forms of argument implied in each dimension of taste. Making judgements of taste, and thus realizing one's reflective taste authority, requires knowledge about which form of knowledge is represented by the dimension of taste in question, and which form of argument can validate a statement, i.e. where one should look for arguments. The students need to know what they are talking about and how to argue for their opinion. It is not enough to state: 'I know' that meatballs taste better than roast pork, when the question of pleasant taste is not a matter of knowledge but of experience. Similarly, the statement: 'In my opinion, fruit is healthy' makes no sense because health is not about 'opinion' but about health-professional knowledge.

This principle can and should be applied to all the seven dimensions of taste identified in Part Two: A System of Taste.

Table 2: Dimensions of taste, knowledge forms and forms of argument

Dimension of taste	Knowledge Form	Form of Argument
Pleasant taste	'I experience'	Aesthetic
Healthy taste	'I know'	Health professional
Sensed taste	'I sense'	Sensory
Moral taste	'It is my opinion'	Normative
Religious taste	'I believe'	Based on faith
Loving taste	'I feel'	Expressive
Trendy taste	'I think'	Based on trend

If the students discuss pleasant taste, the question is whether something tastes pleasant or not. Of course, the starting point is that which is being sensed; however, whether it is salty or sweet does not determine whether the taste is pleasant. Here, the sensory perception must be summarized in an experience: I 'experience' that this tastes amazing or horrible, and the qualification, i.e. form of argument, is aesthetic: how are the different taste elements balanced; how is the food presented; how does the visual impression relate to smell and mouthfeel? All this and much more can be summarized in an aesthetic judgement.

If the students discuss healthy taste, the question is whether something tastes healthy or not. The question of whether marshmallows are healthy must be kept separate from whether they are tasty, unless of course the argument is that satisfying one's sense of tastiness is healthy in itself. Arguments are taken from the health-professional repertoire, and the actualized form of knowledge is informed by professional or research-based knowledge. 'I know that this is healthy' means that there is professional or research evidence to back up the statement.

If the students discuss sensed taste, the question is what they taste: is it salty, sour, sweet, bitter or umami? Whether something is salty is not a matter of opinion but can be determined on the basis of measurable sensory impressions. The discussion of pleasant taste can end with someone liking and someone else disliking something. But whether something is salty can be determined by referring to the sensory argumentation repertoire. The question can be settled objectively, and the discussion cannot end with someone maintaining that 'you might think the potatoes are salty, but I don't'. Whether the potatoes are salty is a question that can be settled with reference to sensory science. Whether they are too salty is a different, aesthetic, matter. Here, the aesthetic taste experience forms the basis for the decision, regardless of whether a consensus is reached.

If the students discuss moral taste, the knowledge form is related to opinion. Here, it is important to distinguish between opinion and feelings. It makes sense to state 'I feel that I love you', as opposed to 'In my opinion, I love you'. On the other hand, it can be our opinion that animal welfare is important, and we can give moral and political reasons for it, whereas we cannot provide valid reasons for 'feeling' that animals should not suffer. 'In my opinion, it is wrong to eat foie gras because the geese suffer when they are force fed' is a viable statement; 'foie gras tastes horrible because the geese suffer' is not. As mentioned earlier in the book, this can give rise to dilemmas because we may have an aesthetic urge to eat something that is produced under morally unacceptable conditions, just like we can feel attracted to the language in the Norwegian author Knut Hamsun's novels despite knowing that he was a Nazi sympathizer. Moral judgements of taste take their arguments from the normative repertoire and are reflected ethically and politically, insofar as political preferences are normatively qualified and ethically reflected.

If the students discuss religious taste, the discussion concerns faith. Whether a ritual meal transcends the world of mundane experience cannot be determined through anything except faith. This applies, for example, to the Christian tradition of communion as it takes place during mass Sunday after Sunday. What is meant by the statement 'this is the body of Christ' cannot be determined by analyzing the ingredients of the host, whether it is salty or not, healthy or not. This does not mean that the ingredients of religious food are of no consequence. Within a symbolic-religious repertoire, e.g. Judaism, it can be of importance whether the bread eaten is leavened or unleavened. However, the arguments are found in theology and knowledge about religious tradition and symbols rather than in gastronomic reference works.

If the students discuss loving taste, feelings take precedence. Meals can be served as expressions of love, for example with candles, smell and taste. Packed lunches are similar from a sensory perspective: they can evoke different feelings of parental love because they express the love that mum or dad put into them. Again, this does not mean that taste is insignificant: it might be the little piece of chocolate next to the carrots that reminds the child of the parent's love. The form of argument is expressive, i.e. based on feelings rather than health science or normative factors.

Finally, if the students discuss trendy taste, it concerns whether food and meals, the way they are served and the context in which they are enjoyed, are trendy. Knowledge is taken from one's sense of fashion and style. One person may say that a pulled duck burger is 'hopelessly old-fashioned', while another may claim that pulled duck is 'amazingly retro in the cool sense'. Whether something tastes good or bad in a gastronomic sense is irrelevant when it comes to trendy taste. Here, a sense of style and current events forms the argument. We think that a certain taste is trendy.

The aim of taste education is for the students to acquire competences, i.e. knowledge about food and meals, and skills to cook, taste and eat meals together. This entails all seven dimensions of taste along with an extensive repertoire of theoretical and practical competences. But it is also the aim of taste education that the students should be stimulated to develop personal taste authority.

Sentire aude

"Sapere aude". This is how Immanuel Kant started his famous article from 1783, which answered the question: "What is Enlightenment?" (Kant 1993 [1783]). Sapere aude: have the courage to use your own understanding. Our invitation is similar, but with a twist because we are not referring to the rational logic of the mind, but the subjective power of judgement related to taste. Sentire aude: have the courage to use your own senses. Offer your opinion. Trust your sense of taste. Know which arguments for taste are valid in which contexts. Commit to presenting your taste experiences in a way that they can be shared with others, and qualified, reflected judgements of taste can be made. How we taste and eat is just as central in a civilization perspective as what we know and think. Meal communities are important contributors to the creation of what Kant called sensus communis, i.e. a community of opinions based on sense, emotion and taste.

Bibliography

Andersen, K. K. (2013). *Kulinarisk Sensorik*. Copenhagen: Erhvervsskolernes Forlag.

Baecker, D. (2006). The Form of the Firm. *Organization: The Critical Journal on Organization, Theory and Society 13*(1), 109-142.

Blixen, K. (1958). *Skæbneanekdoter*. Copenhagen: Gyldendal.

Bourdieu, P. (1979). *La distinction : Critique sociale du jugement*. Paris: Éditi-ions de Minuit.

Brønnum Carlsen, H. & Terndrup Pedersen, A. (2014). *Madkundskab* (1. udgave ed.). Copenhagen: Akademisk Forlag.

Carlsen, H. B. (2017). *Madkundskabsdidaktik*. Copenhagen: Hans Reitzels Forlag.

Carlsen, H. B. & Pedersen, A. T. (2014). *Madkundskab*. Copenhagen: Akademisk Forlag.

Chevrier, F. (2011). *Notre Gastronomie est une culture*. Paris: F. Bourin.

Christensen, J. (2017). *Et videnskabeligt didaktisk perspektiv på madkundskab i skolen med projekt Madkamp som genstandsfelt*. Ph.D.-dissertation. Copenhagen: Aarhus University, DPU – Danish School of Education.

Christensen, J. & Wistoft, K. (2016). "Taste as a didactic approach: enabling students to achieve learning goals". *International Journal of Home Economics* 9(1): 20-34.

Christensen, J., Clark, A. & Wistoft, K. (2018). *Forskningsbaseret evaluering af MIT Kokkeri 2.0*. Copenhagen: Aarhus University, DPU – Danish School of Education.

Comenius, J. A. (1960 [1628-32]). *Grosse Didaktik*. Leipzig: Verlag Helmut Küpper

———. (1910 [1658]). *Orbis Sensualium Pictus*. Leipzig: Druck und Verlag von Julius Klinkhardt.

Durkheim, E. (1915 [1912]). *The Elementary Forms of the Religious Life*. London: George Allen & Unwin.

Dyg, P. M., Wistoft, K. & Lassen, M. C. (2016). *Haver til Maver. Studie af udbredelse og effekter af kulinarisk skolehaveprogram*. Copenhagen: Aarhus University, DPU – Danish School of Education.

Garnier, C. (2001). Les petits français à l'école du Gout. In: *The French Review*, 74 (3): 496-504.

Hattie, J. (2009). *Visible learning: A synthesis of over 800 meta-analyses relating to achievement*. London: Routledge.

Hedegaard, L. (2017). Filosofiske forståelser af smag. In: Hedegaard, L. og Leer, J. (red.). *Perspektiver på smag*. Odense: Taste for Life, # TASTE 5, University of Southern Denmark.

Herbart, J. F. (1964 [1806]). *Allgemeine Pädagogik aus dem Zweck der Erziehung abgeleitet*. In Herbart, J. F. *Sämtliche Werke*. Amsterdam: Scientica Verlag, bd. 2.

Højlund, S. (2015). Taste as a social sense: rethinking taste as a cultural activity. *Flavour* 4:6. http://www.flavourjournal.com/content/4/1/6 (downloaded September 10, 2017).

Højlund, S. (2016). *Smag*. Aarhus: Aarhus University Press.

Hopmann, S. (2007). Restrained Teaching: the common core of Didaktik. *European Educational Research Journal, 6*(2).

Howes, D. (2010). *Sensual relations: Engaging the senses in culture and social theory*. Michigan: University of Michigan Press.

Johnston, J. & Baumann, S (2014). *Foodies: Democracy and distinction in the gourmet foodscape*. London: Routledge.

Juul, J. (1995). *Dit kompetente barn*. Copenhagen: Forlaget Schønberg.

Kant, I. (1971 [1790]). *Kritik der Urteilskraft*. Stuttgart: Reclam (English: Kant, I. (1952). *The Critique of Judgement*. Oxford: Clarendon Press).

———. (2002 [1787]). *Kritik af den rene fornuft*. Copenhagen: Det lille Forlag (English: Kant, I. (2007): *Critique of Pure Reason*. London: Penguin Books).

————. (1993 [1783]). Besvarelse af spørgsmålet: Hvad er oplysning? I Morten Haugaard Jeppesen (red.): *Oplysning, historie, fremskridt*. Copenhagen: Forlaget Slagmark.

Khandelia, H. & Mouritsen, O.G. (2012). Velsmag sådan virker det. *Aktuel Naturvidenskab*. Vol 4: 6-9.

Korsgaard, O., Kristensen, J. E. & Jensen, H. S. (2017). *Pædagogikkens idéhistorie*. Aarhus: Aarhus University Press.

Krogager, H. & I. Olsen ed. (2010). *Ernæring, sundhed og sygdom*. København: Munksgaard Danmark.

Kruse, S. (2006). Udvikling af universitetslærerens pædagogiske kompetencer en didaktisk skitse. *Universitetspædagogisk Tidsskrift, 2*: 36-44.

————. (2007). Hvad konstituerer indholdet i undervisningen? et (fag) didaktisk grundlagsproblem i systemteoretisk belysning. In Schnack (ed.) *Didaktik på kryds og tværs*. Copenhagen: Danish University of Education.

Kruse, S. & Wistoft, K. (2011). Didaktik som forskningsfelt. In Dahl, K. B., Læssøe, J. & Simovska, V. (ed). *Essays om dannelse, didaktik og handlekompetence inspireret af Karsten Schnack*. Copenhagen: Aarhus University, DPU – Danish School of Education.

Leer, J. & Wistoft, K. (2015). *Mod en smagspædagogik: Et kritisk litteratur review om børn, smag og læring*. Odense: Taste for Life, # TASTE 3, University of Southern Denmark.

Lindblad, S. & Sahlström, F. (1999). Gamla mönster och nya gränser. Om ramfaktorer och klassrumsinteraktion. *Pedagogisk Forskning i Sverige* 4(1): 73-92.

Luhmann, N. (1988). *Macht*. Stuttgart: Ferdinand Enke Verlag.

————. (1990). Das Erkenntnisprogramm des Konstruktivismus und die unbekannt bleibende Realität. In Luhmann, N. (ed.). *Soziologische Aufklärung 5*. Opladen: Westdeutscher Verlag.

————. (2000). *Sociale systemer. Grundrids til en almen teori*. Copenhagen: Hans Reitzels Forlag (English: Luhmann, N. (1995). *Social Systems*. Stanford, CA: Stanford University Press).

————. (2000a). *Die Religion der Gesellschaft*. Frankfurt am Main: Suhrkamp Verlag (English: Luhmann, N. (2013). *A Systems Theory of Religion*. Stanford: Stanford University Press).

————. (2006). *Samfundets uddannelsessystem*. Copenhagen: Hans Reitzel (German: Luhmann, N. (2002). *Das Erziehungssystem der Gesellschaft*. Frankfurt am Main: Suhrkamp Verlag).

————. (2012, 2013). *Theory of society, volume 1 and 2*. Stanford, CA: Stanford University Press.

Luhmann, N. & Schoor, K. E. (1988 [1979]). *Reflexionsprobleme im Erziehungssystem*. Frankfurt am Main: Suhrkamp Verlag.

Merleau-Ponty, M. (1945). *Phénoménologie de la perception*. Paris: Éditions Gallimard.

Merton, R. K. (1982). *Social research and the practicing professions*. Abt Books: Cambridge, MA.

Mouritsen, O.G. (2014). Gastrofysik: videnskab, velsmag, velbefindende. In C.R. Kjaer (Ed.), *25 søforklaringer: Naturvidenskabelige fortællinger fra Søauditorierne* (pp. 389). Aarhus: Aarhus University Press.

————. (2015). Smag på naturvidenskaben. *LMKF-bladet*, 1: 32-39.

————. (2016). Gastrophysics of the Oral Cavit. *Current Pharma-ceutical Design*, 22: 2195-2220.

Mouritsen, O.G. & Styrbæk, K. (2015). *Fornemmelse for smag*. Copenhagen: Nyt Nordisk Forlag.

————. (2017). *Mouthfeel: How Texture Makes Taste*. New York: Columbia University Press.

Nyvang, C. (2013). Danske trykte kogebøger 1900-1970. Fire kostmologier. PhD dissertation. Copenhagen: Copenhagen University.

————. (2017). Barnemad: Danske kogebøger til børn, 1847-1975. In Jensen, M. B. og Fabienke, T. N. (ed.): *Ved bordet mennesker, mad & nature morte*, 156-164. Aarhus: Aarhus University Press.

Povlsen, K.K. (2007). Smag, livsstil og madmagasiner. *MedieKultur* 23(42/43): 46-53.

Prescott, J. (2012). *Taste Matters: Why We Like the Food We Do*. London : Reaktion Books.

Puisais, J. & C. Pierre (1987). *Le goût et l'enfant*. Paris: Flammarion.

Qvortrup, A. & Keiding, T. B. (2017). *Undervisning mellem hensigt og uforudsigelighed*. Frederikshavn: Dafolo.

Qvortrup, B. & Qvortrup, L. (2013). *Folkeskolens virkelighed efter konflikten*. Feature article in Politiken, Maj 5, 2013.

Qvortrup, L. (2004). *Det vidende samfund. Mysteriet om viden, læring og dannelse*. Copenhagen: Unge Pædagoger.

———. (2016). *Forskningsinformeret læringsledelse*. Frederikshavn: Dafolo.

Rasmussen, J. (2004). *Undervisning i det refleksivt moderne. Politik, Profession, Pædagogik*. Copenhagen: Hans Reitzels Forlag.

Schmidt, L.-H. (1991). *Smagens analytik*. Aarhus: Modtryk.

Schnack, K. (1992). *Dannelse og demokrati. Udvalgte artikler*. Copenhagen: Danish School of Education.

———. (1998). Handlekompetence. In N. J. Bisgaard (Ed.), *Pædagogiske teorier*. Copenhagen: Billesøe & Baltzer.

Schnack, K. (2007). *Didaktik på kryds og tværs* (1). Copenhagen: Danmarks Pædagogiske Universitetsforlag.

Shepherd, G.M. (2011). *Neurogastronomy*. New York: Columbia University Press.

Sutton, D. & Vournelis, L. (2009). Vefa or Mamalakis: Cooking Up Nostalgia in Contemporary Greece. *South European Society and Politics*. 14(2), 147-166.

Terhart, E. (2003). Constructivism and teaching: A new paradigm in general didactics. *Journal of Curriculum Studies, 35*: 25-44.

Thyssen, O. (2004). *Genkendelsens under en lille bog om iagttagelse*. Copenhagen: Gyldendal.

Von Foerster, H. (1982). *Observing Systems*. California: Intersystems Publications.

Warde, A. (1997). *Consumption, food, and taste. Culinary antinomies and commodity culture*. London: SAGE Publications.

Wistoft, K. (2009). *Sundhedspædagogik viden og værdier*. Copenhagen: Hans Reitzels Forlag.

———. (2012). *Trivsel og selvværd: mental sundhed i skolen* (1. udgave ed.). Copenhagen: Hans Reitzels Forlag.

———. (2013). The desire to learn as a kind of love: gardening, cooking, and passion in outdoor education. *Journal of Adventure Education and Outdoor Learning*, 13(2):125-141.

Wistoft, K. et al. (2011). *Haver til maver. Et studie af engagement, skolehaver og naturformidling*. Copenhagen: Aarhus University, DPU – Danish School of Education.

Wistoft, K., Lassen, M. C. & Christensen, J. (2016). *Evaluering af Mit kokkeri: Del 1 & 2*. Copenhagen: Aarhus University, DPU – Danish School of Education.

Wistoft, K. & Qvortrup, L. (2018a). *Smagens didaktik*. Copenhagen: Akademisk Forlag.

Wistoft, K. & Qvortrup, L. (2018b). When the Kids Conquered the Kitchen: Danish Taste Education and the New Nordic Kitchen. *Gastronomica. The Journal of Critical Food Studies*, 18(4):82-93.

Wittgenstein, L. (1969 [1921]). *Tractatus logico-philosophicus. Logisch-philosophische Abhandling*. Frankfurt am Main: Suhrkamp Verlag. (English: Wittgenstein, L. (1997 [1921]). *Tractatus logico-philosophicus*. London: Dover Publications).

Young, M. (2008). From Constructivism to Realism in the Sociology of the Curriculum. *Review of Research in Education, 32*(1): 1-28.

Children's Cookbooks

Björk, C. (1981). *Linus laver mad*. Copenhagen: Gyldendal.

Brenøe, K. (1974). *Børnenes billedkogebog*. Copenhagen: Chr. Erichsen Forlag.

Broeng, E. (1985). *Grøn mad sund & glad*. Copenhagen: Gyldendals Børnebogklub.

Bubber & Carlsen, L. (2007). *Kloden rundt i Danmark*. Copenhagen: TV 2 Denmark.

Carlsen, H. B. (1998). *Mums kærlighed til sidste bid*. Copenhagen: L&R Fakta.

Disney, W. (1986). *Anders Ands kogebog*. Copenhagen: Wangels Forlag A/S.

———. (1987). *Mickey's kogebog*. Copenhagen: Gutenberghus Gruppen.

Foghsgaard, V. & Lund, L. O. (2009). *Sukkersheriffen. Få styr på familiens sukkervaner.* Copenhagen: Politiken.

Gericke, S. (1990). *Børnekogebog.* Copenhagen: Gyldendalske Boghandel.

Grøndahl, M. og Vinge, T. (2003). *Stjerneguf. Syv af de seje giver dig deres bedste opskrifter.* Copenhagen: Mellemfolkeligt Samvirke.

Hannestad, L. (1982). *Nemt og sjovt mad for unge.* Copenhagen: Forum.

Hansen, C. L. (2016). *Scorekogebogen.* Aarhus: Turbine.

Heiberg, M. (2006). *Heibergs børnedessertcirkus.* Copenhagen: Politikens Forlag.

Høeg-Larsen, K. (1993a). *Lasse og Lærke laver mad.* Aarhus: Forlaget Klematis.

———. (1993b). *Lasse og Lærke bager.* Aarhus: Forlaget Klematis.

Ingemann, D. (2015). *Sukkerfri børnefest is, kager, desserter og søde sager.* Copenhagen: Gyldendal.

Jensen, J. (1994). *Fantasibrød: Børnenes bedste bagebog.* Danmarks 4H. Skejby: 4H-forlaget.

Klinken, K. (2008). *Prinsessekogebogen.* Copenhagen: Politikens Forlag. The Danish Committee for Health Education (2014). *MIT kokkeri* (1 ed.) Copenhagen: The Danish Committee for Health Education.

Larsen, J. U. (1993). *Søde sager for små slikmunde af rene råvarer.* Copenhagen: Forlaget Olivia.

Lunding, C. & Nielsen, C. B. (2011). *Smag til.* Hinnerup: without publishers.

Mangor, M. (1847). *Kogebog for smaa Piger udgivet af en Bedstemoder.* Copenhagen: Own publisher.

Meyer, C. & Poulsen, O. (2000). *Meyers køkkenbørn.* Copenhagen: DR Multimedia.

———. (2001). *Søde sager. Meyers køkkenbørn.* Copenhagen: DR Multimedia.

———. (2002). *Yndlingsmadpakker.* Meyers køkkenbørn. Copenhagen: DR Multimedia.

Nielsen, L. S. (2012). *Lækkerier på larvefødder.* Copenhagen: Forlaget Mellemgaard.

Nielsen, T. & Holmberg, F. (2015). *Vild mad i skolen jagten på de gode råvarer.* Copenhagen: Naturvejledningen i Danmarks Jægerforbund.

Nielsen, V. A. & Sønsthagen, K (1986). *Børnenes grønne kogebog.* Copenhagen: Høst & Søns Forlag.

Nilsson, E. (1987). *Kazoo kogebogen.* Spændende retter som børn kan lave. Copenhagen: Forlagsvirksomheden DR.

Olsen, R., Olsen, F. & Olsen, N. (2016). *Rositas og Franciskas bistro. Om køkkenskills for teens og andre unge som elsker mad og fester.* Copenhagen: People's Press.

Pedersen, K. M. (1982). *Lav selv mad 2, lærervejledning.* Copenhagen: Forum.

Petersen, H. (1973). *Vi laver mad.* Notabenetips 28. Copenhagen: Forlaget Notabene.

Plum, C. (1997). *Ælle, bælle frikadelle.* Copenhagen: Gyldendal.

Skaarup, K. (2012). *Den lille grønne for madpakkespisere.* Copenhagen: Klematis.

Soll, M. & Saly, M. (2015). *Mad i børnehøjde.* Copenhagen: Byens Forlag.

Stenkjær, B. & Eskildsen, U. (1983). *Mad og vilde planter, Hjemkundskab/Biologi 6-10. skoleår.* Aarhus: Pædagogisk Forlag, Hjemkundskab.

Søby, A., Søby I-M & Larsen, E. (2006). *Jubii jeg har maddag.* Odense: Forlaget Mellemgaard.

Söderqvist, Å. & Åberg, L. (1971). *Børnenes kokkebog.* Copenhagen: Høst & Søn.

Thomsen, H. F. & Dørge, B. (1983). *Børnenes kogeog bagebog, og også ungkarlenes.* Copenhagen: Politikens Forlag.

Thorhauge, C. & Hundebøll, B. (2014). *Ønskebørns yndlingsretter.* Kys kræsenhed farvel. Copenhagen: Muusmann forlag.

Wilkes, A. (1991a). *Min første kogebog.* Copenhagen: Gyldendal.

———. (1991b). *Min første festbog.* Copenhagen: Gyldendal.

Østergaard, L. & Bachmann, P. (2016). *Venindekogebogen.* Copenhagen: Politikens Forlag.

Other Sources

Anima (2014). https://anima.dk/landbrugsdyr/br%C3%B8drene-pri-ce-f%C3%A6rdige-med-foie-gras#. WWSQ72ZlIdU (downloaded July 11, 2017).

Bologna-process. https://ufm.dk/uddannelse/internationalisering/internationalt-samarbejde-om-uddannelse/
bologna-processen/bologna-processen (downloaded February 1, 2019).

Copenhagen Street Food (2017). http://copenhagenstreetfood.dk/stader/ (downloaded July 12, 2017).

Dede, C. (2009). *Comparing Frameworks for "21st Century Skills"*. Harvard Graduate School of Education.http://sttechnology.pbworks.com/f/ (downloaded February 1, 2019).

Dede_(2010)_Comparing%20Frameworks%20for%2021st%20Century%20Skills.pdf (downloaded February 1, 2019).

Dyrenes beskyttelse (2017). https://www.dyrenesbeskyttelse.dk/mad-for-brug#lGPB5LBFB74ABL pM.99 (downloaded July 10, 2017).

EMU.DK/modul/madkundskab-fælles-mål-læseplan-og-vejledning Danmarks Læringsportal. http://www.emu.dk/modul/madkundskab-fæl-les-mål-læseplan-og-vejledning.dk/modul/
Madkundskab-f%C3%A6l-les-m%C3%A5l-l%C3%A6seplan-og-vejledning (downloaded September 10, 2017).

Gastromand (2015). https://gastromand.dk/opskrift-foie-gras-terrine/ (downloaded July 10, 2017).

Gunnars, K. (2018). https://www.healthline.com/nutrition/10-proven-benefits-of-kale (downloaded June 23, 2019).

Information (2000). https://www.information.dk/2007/07/foie-gras-hyk-leriet (downloaded July 11, 2017).

http://politiken.dk/mad/madnyt/art4981482/Pri-ce-br%C3%B8dre-forsvarer-foie-gras-spisning (downloaded 11, 2017).

Price (2010). https://www.dr.dk/mad/opskrift/foie-gras-terrine and https://www.dr.dk/mad/opskrift/stegt-foie-gras-med-salat-af-puy-linser-aeble-persillerod-og (downloaded July 11, 2017).

Ryman, E. (2015) http://www.smagforlivet.dk/artikler/fed-smag-velkommen-til-den-sjette-grundsmag (downloaded June 23, 2019).

Undervisningsministeriet (2017). https://www.emu.dk/modul/madkundskab-f%C3%A6lles-m%C3%A5l-l%C3%A6seplan-og-vejledning (downloaded July 11, 2017).

Teaching Taste

Dimensions of Taste — Teaching Handout

PROPOSAL FOR A DIDACTIC TASTE SYSTEM

Method

Our general objective is to present a systematic model for qualifying reflections on taste education. Thus, this presentation features empirically informed theoretical work. It aims to push the boundaries of theory and research in order to seek out a new food education paradigm, including a model of seven basic dimensions of taste. Based on this model, we suggest new ways of framing taste or food education.

The starting point for our research is curriculum development (Leer and Wistoft 2015) and empirical, effectiveness-oriented research in Home Economics education (Christensen and Wistoft 2016). This is combined with systems theory developed by the German sociologist Niklas Luhmann (Luhmann 1995 [1984]), which is used to inform concepts for the different dimensions of a didactics of taste and their interrelations conceptualized as 'structural couplings' (Luhmann

2012, 2013 [1997]). Luhmann's concepts have been transformed from a general theory on society to a taste didactic reflection theory. In other words, we have transferred theory and concepts from one area to another, just like, e.g., the concept of 'autopoiesis' can be transferred from biology to sociology (Luhmann 1984).

Furthermore, each of the seven dimensions of our taste system is inspired by a broad range of philosophical, theoretical and practical input, including concepts from the philosophy of aesthetics (Kant 1973 (1793)), health education and practice (Wistoft 2009, 2013), natural science (Mouritsen and Styrbæk 2014 and 2016; Shepherd 2011) and moral philosophy (Kant 1973 [1788]).

SEVEN DIMENSIONS OF TASTE: AN EXAMPLE

What do we mean, when we say that something tastes 'good'? Recently, we prepared and served a fish dish, and we identified seven dimensions:

1. We taste aesthetically and think that the fish tastes good and it is a pleasure to eat;

2. we taste in relation to health and are pleased that fish is healthy (regarding proteins and omega-3 and 6) and that it is healthy to have time for each other in connection with the meal;

3. we use our sense of sight, hearing, smell, touch (mouthfeel) and taste, i.e. the entire sensory repertoire;

4. we discuss organic fish farming, fishing and sustainability when we conclude with pleasure that the fish tastes good because it is organic and caught 'locally';

5. we activate our religious taste, thinking that the meal is heavenly;

6. we clearly sense that the food is prepared with love and experience the taste of a loving meal;

7. we agree that by serving and eating food in this way, we are trendy in the manner of celebrities

SEVEN DIMENSIONS OF TASTE: A TABLE

If we arrange the seven dimensions in a table, it may look as follows:

Dimension of taste	What is it about?	What kind of knowledge do we need?
Pleasant taste	Pleasure	Aesthetics, incl. gastronomy
Healthy taste	Well-being and nutrition	Knowledge about health, incl. nutritional science
Sensed taste	Sensory perception	Knowledge about sensory perception, incl. sensory science
Moral taste	Social norms	Ethics, incl. food ethics
Religious taste	Faith	Knowledge about faith, incl. religious food and meal rituals

Loving taste	Love/ passion	Knowledge about love articulated through food/ meals
Trendy taste	Style	Knowledge about fashion and style, expressed through food/ meals

Let's go through all the seven dimensions of taste, one by one.

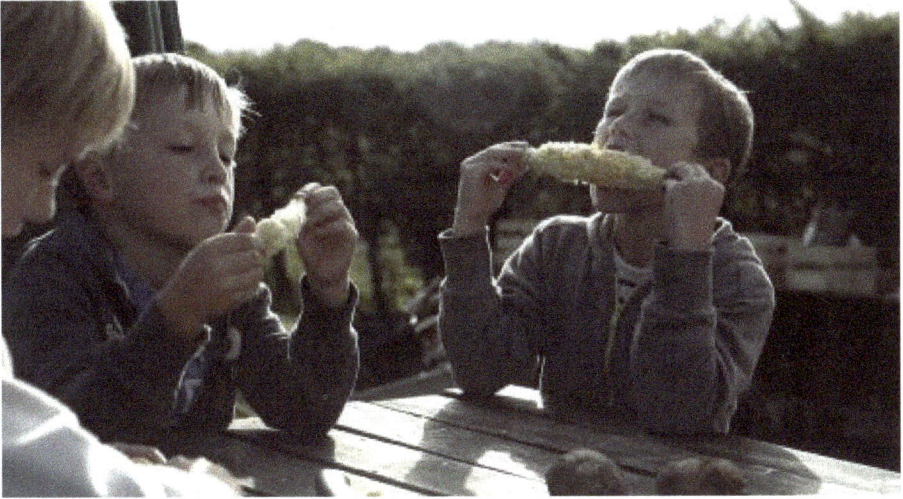

PLEASANT TASTE

Dimension of taste	What is it about?	What kind of knowledge do we need?
Pleasant taste	Pleasure. Is it delicious or does it taste bad?	Aesthetics, incl. gastronomy

In Denmark, the trend towards an aesthetic kitchen was launched in 2000 with Claus Meyer's and Ole Poulsen's book "Meyer's Kitchen Children".

The intention behind the book was presented as follows:

> We believe that in the long run, the joy of cooking and eating together is best developed when children experience that food is something that is prepared with a certain measure of gastronomic enthusiasm for the pleasure of oneself and others. We believe in the significance of challenging from the very beginning children's taste buds and stimulating their desire to explore the possibilities and mysteries of cooking (Meyer & Poulsen, 2000: 4).

Discussion

Think of a meal you've had or prepared recently: What does it mean that something tastes good or bad, and how does it manifest itself in the taste?

It is well known that it is difficult to substantiate whether and why something tastes good or bad. But try this three-step model:

1. Do you like or do you dislike the taste? This is the first step: "I like or I dislike lasagna"

2. Now you have to substantiate your judgment: What does it remind you of? For instance, the taste of lasagna may remind you of Italy, nice weather and big families.

3. Finally, you have to understand that your opinion isn´t shared by everyone. Who shares your opinion, and who doesn't? In one culture, crispy pork cracklings are a delicacy, whereas in another, pork is abominable. (It is important that the students learn that this is the case).

HEALTHY TASTE

Dimension of taste	What is it about?	What kind of knowledge do we need?
Healthy taste	Well-being and nutrition. Does it taste healthy or unhealthy?	Knowledge about health and nutrition, incl. knowledge about personal and social well-being and nutritional science

Healthy taste can be viewed in a dual perspective: well-being and nutrition.

Health in a Well-being Perspective

Well-being is linked to personal involvement and social food and meal values. If meal communities are built on joy of life, equality and social responsibility, they can contribute to furthering social well-being.

Well-being signifies a comfortable feeling that involves energy, drive, resolve and positive experience in cooking and eating with others.

Health in a Nutrition Perspective

The other aspect is related to the nutritional health concept. We can work with nutrition on the basis of the three main sources of energy: protein, fat and carbohydrates in connection with groups of food, which makes the sources easier to recognize in their everyday forms. But we also have to include vitamins, fatty acids and minerals, as well as energy demand and balance.

Discussion

Think of a meal you've had or prepared recently: What does it mean that something tastes healthy or unhealthy? Try to use these three approaches in your discussion:

1. digestion and factors influencing the energy demand;

2. the impact of carbohydrates, fats, proteins, fatty acids, fibers, vitamins and minerals on illness and health;

3. the content of energy, energy-providing nutrients, fatty acids, fibers and significant contents of vitamins and minerals in different foods.

SENSED TASTE

Dimension of taste	What is it about?	What kind of knowledge do we need?
Sensed taste	Sensory perception. Does it give you a sense experience or not?	Knowledge about sensory perception, incl. sensory science

When we talk about sensed taste, we are dealing with a dimension of taste that brings the discussion in a sensory and physical/ chemical direction. In other words, sensed taste regards the sense of taste, i.e. the complex connections between the biological taste buds, the associated biochemical processes and the psychological sense experiences.

The sense buds are sensitive towards the five different basic flavors: sour, sweet, salty, bitter and umami. However, the sensed taste cannot be reduced to this description because it will always be a result of an integrated multisensory process in the brain that encompasses chemical taste, smell, mouthfeel, sight and hearing. Further, it does not make sense to perceive the experience of taste as merely a sensory-physiological occurrence. It also always has a social, psychological and cultural dimension that is connected to norms, education, lifestyle, aesthetics, values and identity.

Discussion

Think of a meal you've had or prepared recently: What does it mean that it gave you a sense experience? Try to use the following three approaches in your discussion and when you practice basic methods of cooking and preparation, i.e. boiling, frying, thickening, baking, grinding and preserving:

1.   identify the basic flavors: sour, sweet, salty, bitter and umami;

2.   combine the additional dimensions of flavor: Not just taste, but also smell, mouthfeel, sight and hearing;

3.   put all the dimensions of flavor into a social, psychological and cultural perspective.

MORAL TASTE

Dimension of taste	What is it about?	What kind of knowledge do we need?
Moral taste	Social norms. Is the taste morally or politically acceptable or not?	Ethics, incl. food ethics

Here, we distinguish between what is morally right and wrong. We develop taste norms. It tastes 'right' to eat sustainable products, whereas it leaves us with a 'bad' taste in our mouth to eat foods produced under socially unacceptable conditions. Eggs are a good example: should we make our omelet from cheap, conventionally produced eggs or choose the ones from free-range chickens? It is hard to tell whether our family will be able to taste the difference, but do you agree that eggs from chickens who have roamed around in a field will give a better 'gut feeling' and therefore better taste?

Taste norms can, in turn, form the basis of taste policy, i.e. politically binding decisions of what we can and cannot eat, or what is imposed with high or low taxes. In the US, taste politics often deal with food justice. In Denmark, taste politics are primarily linked to health policy: alcohol, cigarettes and sugar-rich products are tax liable. In other countries, good taste is also rewarded, e.g. in South Korea, where 'the Korean cow' is protected by practically banning the import of beef. Another example is France, where all schools work one week a year with 'La semaine du goût' [the taste and flavor week]. Here, the students learn to distinguish between French gastronomy and, for example, ketchup, burgers and other types of foreign food.

Discussion

Think of a meal you've had or prepared recently: Try to evaluate it from the point of view of food morals. Should we avoid eating food from animals that have suffered, or fruit, coffee, etc. from farms with bad working conditions?

1. Is there something that leaves you with a 'bad taste'?

2. Try to generalize: When are certain foods ethically acceptable, and when are they not?

3. Should certain foods be politically banned?

RELIGIOUS TASTE

Dimension of taste	What is it about?	What kind of knowledge do we need?
Religious taste	Faith. Does the taste of the meal have a spiritual dimension or not? Does it have an 'us/ them' function?	Knowledge about faith, incl. religious food and meal rituals

We can distinguish between two different ways of talking about religious taste. One takes its point of departure in food and meals with a focus on the transcendent effect of the meal or dish. When you eat something that is cooked to religious taste, it gives you a spiritual experience. One example is the Christians communion, which is repeated during church services, where the celebrant at the altar refers to the bread as 'the body of Christ' and the wine as 'the blood of Christ': Eating a piece of bread and drinking a tiny glass of wine gives you the feeling of getting closer to God.

The other way focuses on the function of food or meals as a ritual community, which—with reference to God and/or a holy principle—creates religious identity. Many people in Denmark, who are not particularly religious, still eat a Christmas meal, because it is rooted in cultural history and gives them a feeling of belonging to a cultural community. It seems that all religions have a relationship to food, and food plays an important role in religious contexts, both in the spiritual sense and in the sense of creating a social or cultural identity.

Discussion

Based on examples from your own background—for instance, your family background—compare food and meal cultures from different religions, eras and places. Try to identify and discuss:

1. What is 'right' and 'wrong' in terms of eating in a particular religious context?

2. What is the social significance of a religious meal: Does it create social identity? Or does it create trust, e.g. does it have a spiritual dimension?

LOVING TASTE

Dimension of taste	What is it about?	What kind of knowledge do we need?
Loving taste	Love/ passion. Does the taste or the meal have a love or passion dimension?	Knowledge about love articulated through food/ meals

Meals are not only about nutrition and hygiene but just as much about love and responsiveness. The love relation represented by the meal can go two ways. First, it can be a relation between the one who cooks the meal and the one or more people who eat it. The chef or the person cooking uses the food and the meal as a medium to express their love. The food and meal constitute a declaration of love expressed through taste. Second, the food and meal make up a framework for a love relation between those who eat.

The meal can be a framework for e.g. parental love or romantic seduction. The food, meal and presentation let the receiver sense (taste, see, smell, hear and feel) whether the cook has expressed love. For example, love—of children, friends and family—can be expressed through daily cooking or crammed into the children's packed lunches.

Loving taste is a result of both individual dishes and meal communities. In terms of taste, the taste elements need to be balanced so that the dish is not too hot, bitter, sour or salty, and the mouthfeel should be soft and seductive. The community should be intimate and arranged to avoid distracting elements. A popular example is the meal in Walt Disney's Lady and the Tramp: Spaghetti Bolognese served under a starlit sky, and with an accordion-playing chef in the background, creates a framework for seduction, and the food is bursting with love for the eating guests.

Discussion

Think of a meal you've had or prepared recently: Try to evaluate it from the point of view of love and passion:

1. Did it have a love dimension?

2. Are there certain ingredients, tastes or recipes that incarnate love? Try to identify them.

TRENDY TASTE

Dimension of taste	What is it about?	What kind of knowledge do we need?
Trendy taste	Style. Is the taste or meal trendy or old-fashioned?	Knowledge about fashion and style expressed through food/ meals

Something is trendy because it represents a style associated with the present. Something is not trendy if it is seen as representative of yesterday's style—or that of last year or last decade. This is also the case with ingredients, taste and meals. Some ingredients appear old-fashioned, while others are really trendy. But looking back, what was trendy two years ago is just as old-fashioned today.

Also, chefs, restaurants, food writers, so-called 'foodies' and street food venues may be trendy or old-fashioned. In Denmark and the Nordic countries, the so-called New Nordic Kitchen has been trendy for about ten years, using local ingredients and preparing them in a way that taps into the regional traditions. However, in Denmark, just twenty years ago, trendy food was Italian or Spanish food, followed—ten years ago—by Japanese food, especially sushi.

Discussion

Try to find an example of a trendy food culture or a trendy meal or taste. Discuss:

1. Why is that meal particularly trendy?

2. Is it part of a general trend?

3.   When will it become old-fashioned?

REASONING ABOUT TASTE

It is not enough to be able to identify the seven dimensions of taste. We also need to know how to reason about taste, because this is important in a cultivated meal community. We can't simply say, "I *know* that this tastes good", because 'good taste' is a question of individual judgment, i.e. a question of personal experience. In comparison, we *know* that something is healthy because we can refer to scientific knowledge concerning well-being and nutrition.

To help you participate in a social discussion on taste, we suggest the following table presenting forms of knowledge and arguments related to each dimension of taste. The ideal is to become able to use your judgment of taste and thereby become a confident and reflecting authority of taste.

Dimension of taste	Knowledge form	Form of argument
Pleasant taste	'I experience'	Aesthetic
Healthy taste	'I know'	Health professional
Sensed taste	'I sense'	Sensory
Moral taste	'It is my opinion'	Normative
Religious taste	'I believe'	Based on faith
Loving taste	'I feel'	Expressive
Trendy taste	'I think'	Based on trend

www.ingramcontent.com/pod-product-compliance
Lightning Source LLC
Chambersburg PA
CBHW040422110426
42814CB00008B/332